100% COTTON YARN

HELLO

AMIGURUMI PEOPLE

16 WONDERFUL CHARACTERS TO CROCHET

LEARN A NEW TECHNIQUE WITH EACH DOLL YOU MAKE

MEI LI LEE

Tuva Publishing

www.tuvapublishing.com

Address Merkez Mah. Cavusbasi Cad. No 71
Cekmekoy - Istanbul 34782 / Turkey
Tel +9 0216 642 62 62

Amigurumi People

First Print 2023 / August

All Global Copyrights Belong To
Tuva Tekstil ve Yayıncılık Ltd.

Content Crochet

Editor in Chief Ayhan DEMİRPEHLİVAN

Project Editor Kader DEMİRPEHLİVAN

Designers Mei Li Lee

Technical Editor Leyla ARAS

Graphic Designers Ömer ALP, Abdullah BAYRAKÇI,
Tarık TOKGÖZ, Yunus GÜLDOĞAN

Photography Tuva Publishing, Mei Li Lee

Illustrations Mei Li Lee

Crochet Tech Editor Wendi CUSINS

ISBN 978-605-7834-61-4

 TuvaYayincilik  TuvaPublishing

 TuvaYayincilik  TuvaPublishing

INTRODUCTION

HELLO, MY DEAREST FRIENDS!

I am so glad to be meeting you here. It has been more than 10 years since I first discovered the world of amigurumi, and I've never been more fascinated by it than now. There's still so much joy left for me to uncover, and this book is only the beginning of another journey.

I can't begin to thank Tuva Publishing enough for believing in me over the years and keeping the door wide open for my original amigurumi designs, and finally saying "yes" to the birth of this book!

My family - my biggest love - has been amazing in showing their support in every little way. I am confident in my creations only because they have made me so. My husband, with his constant encouragement to make time to craft my own path in dreams. My two older boys, with their "Yes, this color" opinions whenever I'm stumped for inspiration. I can't help but get supercharged with renewed energy whenever they say: "Mommy, that doll looks really nice!", and then proceed to ask when I will be available to make one more (actually, one each) for them.

To my littlest one, who was snug as a bug in my tummy when I first started working on this book — thank you for all the days of good naps (and many more to come, I hope!) so Mommy could work on making more wonderful amigurumi.

I can't wait for you to meet the 16 friends I have gathered for you in this book. They come from all walks of life, each with a story to tell. I hope you will like them as much as I do, and take them by hand into your own world of amigurumi.

May crochet bring you peace and purpose and reignite your imagination to see things with a child-like wonder. I know it has for me.

MEI

PROJECT GALLERY

SLEEPY-TIME SOPHIE
P.24

HELENA THE DOCTOR
P. 32

OLLIE THE FIREFIGHTER
P. 40

AUSTIN THE ASTRONAUT & ROCKET
P.50

MEGAN THE EXCHANGE STUDENT
P.60

ANNA THE BALLERINA
P.68

GRANDPA & GRANDMA
P.76

BEST FRIENDS
P.88

MOMMY & TWINS
P.100

ZARA THE ZOOKEEPER & ELEPHANT
P.118

LITTLE SCOTTIE
P.128

SAMANTHA THE BIG SISTER
P.136

CONTENTS

PROJECTS

MATERIALS
&
TOOLS

. . . .

CROCHET
&
AMIGURUMI BASICS

MATERIALS

Important Safety Note

If you plan to make the dolls in this book for babies and children under the age of three, you can make these adjustments to ensure that they are safe for the little ones:

1) Substitute the safety eyes and scrapbooking brads with embroidery stitches or a crochet piece.
2) Replace all buttons with circular crochet pieces.
3) Go over your whipstitches twice when sewing on a limb or accessories, making sure there are no loose parts that could come undone and may pose a choking hazard.

Yarn

HELLO Cotton Yarn is my latest go-to yarn of choice for making amigurumi. I really love the range of colors available and also how smoothly it slides on the hook without splitting.

Matte cotton yarns are my favorite, as it gives amigurumi an aged, vintage look that is so unique to handmade dolls.

PS It is perfectly fine to substitute the yarn used in this book with a yarn of your choice. Just remember to adjust the hook size accordingly.

Hooks

Indeed, not all hooks are made equal. Pairing your yarn with the right hook is absolutely necessary to make the amigurumi-making journey more enjoyable. I love the Clover Amour and also the Clover Soft Touch hooks, and I have one each in every size.

They are a good investment to make if you plan to crochet for a long time, as they can last for many years.

To know which hook size to pair with your yarn, try going one size smaller than the recommended hook size as shown on the yarn label. This will give you tighter stitches, and your amigurumi will be less likely to have "holes" with stuffing peeking through.

Hook Size Conversion Table

Metric	U.S.	UK/Canada
2.25 mm	B-1	13
2.75 mm	C-2	12
3.00 mm	-	11
3.25 mm	D-3	10
3.50 mm	E-4	-
3.75 mm	F-5	9
4.00 mm	G-6	8
4.50 mm	7	7
5.00 mm	H-8	6
5.50 mm	I-9	5
6.00 mm	J-10	4
6.50 mm	K-10 ½	3

Stuffing

Polyester fiberfill (also known as polyfill or fiberfill) is what I use for all my amigurumi. It is soft and fluffy and does not clump.

Good stuffing will give your amigurumi an even shape. I usually use the back of my Clover Amour hooks to push the stuffing in, especially for narrower pieces.

The Stitch Markers

When I first started crocheting, I didn't know about stitch markers and kept losing count of my rounds and had to start over multiple times. Locking stitch markers that don't fall out easily are absolutely necessary for beginners. A good substitute would be a safety pin or a paperclip.

Yarn Needle

This is one of the most important tools to have in your crochet bag as you will need to use it at least once during your amigurumi work, either to weave in ends or to sew different parts together. Find one that has an eye large enough to pass your yarn through. I use a blunt-tipped metal needle, but you can also try a bent-tip needle, or one made out of plastic.

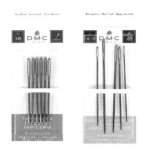

Safety Eyes

Safety eyes come in a variety of sizes and are commonly circular or oval in shape. They need to be locked in place before you stuff and close up your amigurumi piece, so it is important to plan ahead on where you want the position of the eyes to be.

Once they are attached, the only way to remove them is to cut away on the locking washer at the back of the eye with a pair of pliers (which means you will need an extra set of washers if you wish to re-attach them).

Scrapbooking Brads

Unlike safety eyes, scrapbooking brads can be easily taken out and moved around on your amigurumi piece. Each brad comes with two prongs at the back that you can bend open to "lock" it in place.

They are usually made of metal and come in all colors, shapes and sizes and have either a shiny or matte appearance. You can find them in craft stores that sell scrapbooking materials.

I've used scrapbooking brads in place of buttons or as eyes and noses. (They can even add a cute pop of color to the cheeks, if you can find the pink ones.)

Embroidery Floss

I like to switch to DMC Embroidery Floss whenever I sew the facial features on my amigurumi. The result is that much more delicate, and the thinner thread makes it easier to form "curves" for lips and eyebrows.

I also like to pair a 2mm crochet hook with the embroidery floss to make mini versions of crochet pieces, like the mini Granny Squares we will make for the baby carrier in the Big Sister pattern.

Fabrics

If you are experienced in sewing, adding fabric garments to your dolls can greatly enhance the look of your amigurumi. I prefer to crochet the clothes, so I only used a small amount of tulle to add texture to the skirt in the Ballerina pattern.

Sewing Needle & Thread

I always keep a sewing needle and some thread in my crochet bag as you never know when you will need to use them for sewing on buttons and beads or strips of fabric.

Other Materials

Small scissors

Straight Pins

Mini Buttons

Beads

Jewelry Wire

Craft Glue

CROCHET TERMINOLOGY

This book uses US crochet terminology.

Basic conversion chart

US	UK
slip stitch (sl st)	slip stitch (sl st)
chain (ch)	chain (ch)
single crochet (sc)	double crochet (dc)
double crochet (dc)	treble crochet (tr)
half-double crochet (hdc)	half treble (htr)
treble (triple) crochet (tr)	double treble (dtr)

Abbreviations Of The Basic Stitches

ch	Chain Stitch
sl st	Slip Stitch
sc	Single Crochet Stitch
hdc	Half-Double Crochet Stitch
dc	Double Crochet Stitch
tr	Treble (or Triple) Crochet Stitch

Standard Symbols Used in Patterns

[ ]	Work instructions within brackets as many times as directed
( )	Work instructions within parentheses in same stitch or space indicated
*	Repeat the instructions following the single asterisk as directed
**	1) Repeat instructions between asterisks as many times as directed; or 2) Repeat from a given set of instructions

Concise Action Terms

dec	Decrease (reduce by one or more stitches)
inc	Increase (add one or more stitches)
join	Join two stitches together, usually with a slip stitch. (Either to complete the end of a round or when introducing a new ball or color of yarn)
rep	Repeat (the previous marked instructions)
turn	Turn your crochet piece so you can work back for the next row/ round
yo	Yarn over the hook. (Either to pull up a loop or to draw through the loops on hook)

CROCHET BASICS

Slip Knot

Almost every crochet project starts with a slip knot on the hook. This is not mentioned in any pattern – it is assumed.

To make a slip knot, form a loop with your yarn (the tail end hanging behind your loop); insert the hook through the loop, and pick up the ball end of the yarn. Draw yarn through loop. Keeping loop on hook, gently tug the tail end to tighten the knot. Tugging the ball end tightens the loop.

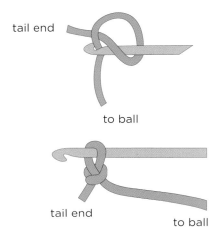

tail end

to ball

tail end

to ball

Yarn Over (yo)

This is a common practice, especially with the taller stitches. With a loop on your hook, wrap the yarn (attached to the ball) from back to front around the shaft of your hook.

Chain Stitch (ch)

The chain stitch is the foundation of most crochet projects. The foundation chain is a series of chain stitches in which you work the first row of stitches.

To make a chain stitch, you start with a slip knot (or loop) on the hook. Yarn over and pull the yarn through the loop on your hook (first chain stitch made). For more chain stitches, repeat: Yarn over, pull through loop on hook.

Hint Don't pull the stitches too tight, otherwise they will be difficult to work in. When counting chain stitches, do not count the slip knot, nor the loop on the hook. Only count the number of 'v's.

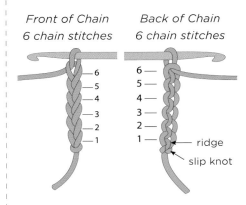

Front of Chain
6 chain stitches

Back of Chain
6 chain stitches

ridge

slip knot

Slip Stitch (sl st)

Starting with a loop on your hook, insert hook in stitch or space specified and pull up a loop, pulling it through the loop on your hook as well.

The slip stitch is commonly used to attach new yarn and to join rounds.

Attaching a New Color or New Ball of Yarn or Joining with a Slip Stitch (join with sl st)

Make a slip knot with the new color (or yarn) and place loop on hook. Insert hook from front to back in the (usually) first stitch (unless specified otherwise). Yarn over and pull loop through stitch and loop on hook (slip stitch made).

Single Crochet (sc)

Starting with a loop on your hook, insert hook in stitch or space specified and draw up a loop (two loops on hook). Yarn over and pull yarn through both the loops on your hook (first sc made).

The height of a single crochet stitch is one chain high.

When working single crochet stitches into a foundation chain, begin the first single crochet in the second chain from the hook. The skipped chain stitch provides the height of the stitch.

At the beginning of a single crochet row or round, start by making one chain stitch (to get the height) and work the first single crochet stitch into first stitch.

Note: *The one chain stitch is never counted as a single crochet stitch.*

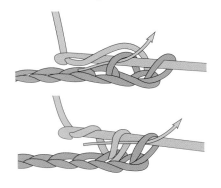

Half-Double Crochet (hdc)

Starting with a loop on your hook, yarn over hook before inserting hook in stitch or space specified and draw up a loop (three loops on hook). Yarn over and pull yarn through all three loops (first hdc made).

The height of a half-double crochet stitch is two chains high.

When working half-double crochet stitches into a foundation chain, begin the first stitch in the third chain from the hook. The two skipped chains provide the height. When starting a row or round with a half-double crochet stitch, make two chain stitches and work in the first stitch.

Note: The two chain stitches are never counted as a half-double stitch.

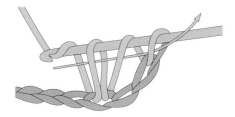

Double Crochet (dc)

Starting with a loop on your hook, yarn over hook before inserting hook in stitch or space specified and draw up a loop (three loops on hook). Yarn over and pull yarn through two loops (two loops remain on hook). Yarn over and pull yarn through remaining two loops on hook (first dc made).

The height of a double crochet stitch is three chains high.

When working double crochet stitches into a foundation chain, begin the first stitch in the fourth chain from the hook.

The three skipped chains count as the first double crochet stitch. When starting a row or round with a double crochet stitch, make three chain stitches (which count as the first double crochet), skip the first stitch (under the chains) and work a double crochet in the next (second) stitch. On the following row or round, when you work in the 'made' stitch, you will be working in the top chain (3rd chain stitch of the three chains).

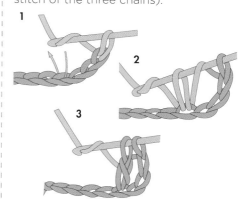

General Information for Making Amigurumi

Choosing the Hook

Use a hook which is a size or two smaller than what is recommended on the yarn label. The fabric created should be tight enough so that the stuffing does not show through the stitches.

Right Side vs Wrong Side of the Fabric

It is important to be able to distinguish between the 'right' (front) and 'wrong' (back) side of the crocheted fabric.

Right Side

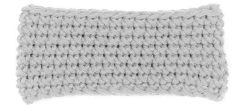

Wrong Side

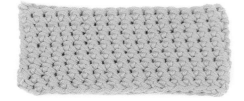

When working in a spiral or joined round, the right side of the fabric is always facing you. Working in rows or turned rounds, it will alternate between 'right' and 'wrong' side.

Single Crochet Rows

Working in a Spiral

Most of the amigurumi pieces are worked in a continuous spiral to create the dimensional shapes needed. Working in a spiral means that at the end of a round, you do not join (or close) with a slip stitch into the first stitch of the round. When you get to the end of the round, you start the next round by just working a stitch into the next stitch (which is the first stitch of the previous round).

Working in Joined (Closed) Rounds

Some parts of an amigurumi pattern might have 'joined rounds'. This is where, at the end of the round, you join with a slip stitch in the first stitch of the round. The next round starts with a number of chain stitches (based on height of the stitches used), and then you continue working stitches for the next round.

Note Do not turn at the end of each joined round, unless instructed to do so.

Working in Rows

For some accessories or patches for your amigurumi, you will need to work in rows. Each row starts by turning the piece and working some chain stitches (known as the 'turning chain'). The number of chain stitches worked is based on the height of the stitches used.

ADAPTING THE DESIGN

There are many ways you can make your amigurumi toy unique.

Size By choosing a different weight yarn, you can make your toys either bigger (using thicker yarn) or smaller (using thinner yarn or thread). Remember to change your hook size too.

Colors This is the easiest way to make your toy unique. Select colors to match décor or personal preference.

Characteristics Changing the facial features of toys, gives them a whole new character. Adding (or removing) embellishments to the overall toy can change the whole look of it.

Eyes Changing the size or color of the eyes can create a totally different facial expression. Instead of using safety eyes, you can use buttons or beads for eyes. If there is a safety concern, you can sew on small bits of felt or embroider the features.

Appliquē patches Whether they are crocheted, fabric or felt (or a combination of these), adding appliqué patches to your doll is a great way to make your toys distinctive. They can be facial features, such as eyes, noses, mouths, cheeks, and maybe even ears. You can also make novelty appliqué patches to use as embellishment on the toys. For example – flowers on a dress, eye-patch for a pirate, overall patch for a farmer.

Embroidery By adding embroidery stitches to the face, (straight stitch, back stitch, etc.) or fancy ones (satin stitch, French knot, bullion stitch, etc.), your toy will take on a personality of its own. You can also use the cross-stitch technique to create a unique look.

Note Embroider all facial features to make a child-safe toy.

Adding Accessories To create your one-of-a-kind toy, you can add various decorations to them. Colored buttons can be used in a variety of ways to spice things up. Using small ribbons and bows can feminize dolls. Attaching a small bunch of flowers or small basket to a doll's hand, tells a new story.

However you choose to give your toy character, each one ends up being unique!

SPECIAL CROCHET STITCHES

Single Crochet Decreases

a) Normal Single Crochet Decrease (dec)

1. Insert hook in specified stitch or space and pull up a loop (2 loops on hook).

2. Insert hook in following stitch or space and pull up a loop (3 loops on hook).

3. Yarn over and draw through all 3 loops on hook.

Single crochet decrease stitch made.

b) Invisible Single Crochet Decrease (inv-dec)

1. Insert hook under the front loop of each of the next 2 stitches.

2. Pull yarn through these two stitch loops (2 loops on hook).

3. Yarn over and draw through both loops on hook.

Invisible single crochet decrease stitch made.

Designer's Note: *I usually use the invisible decrease when working in rounds, for a neater look.*

Double Crochet Decrease (dc2tog)

1. Yarn over hook, insert into next stitch and pull up a loop. (3 loops on hook).

2. Yarn over and draw through 2 loops on hook (2 loops remain on hook).

3. Yarn over hook, insert into following stitch and pull up a loop (4 loops on hook).

4. Yarn over and draw through 2 loops on hook (3 loops remain on hook).

5. Yarn over and draw through remaining 3 loops on hook.

Double crochet decrease stitch made.

Treble Crochet (tr)

1. Yarn over hook twice, insert into next stitch and pull up a loop (4 loops on hook).

2. Yarn over and draw through first 2 loops on hook (3 loops remain on hook).

3. Yarn over and draw through 2 loops on hook (2 loops remain on hook).

4. Yarn over and draw through remaining 2 loops on hook.

Treble crochet stitch made.

Bobble Stitch (bob)

This decorative stitch creates a puffy bump on the surface of your amigurumi. It can be used to add texture on a piece of clothing. I used it to make the thumb bump on the astronaut's gloves, and also as the arms and legs on Sleepy-Time Sophie bunny stuffy toy.

1. Yarn over hook, insert into next stitch and pull up a loop (3 loops on hook).

2. Yarn over and draw through 2 loops on hook (2 loops remain on hook).

3. Yarn over hook, insert into same stitch and pull up a loop (4 loops on hook).

4. Yarn over and draw through 2 loops on hook (3 loops on hook).

5. Yarn over hook, insert into same stitch and pull up a loop (5 loops on hook).

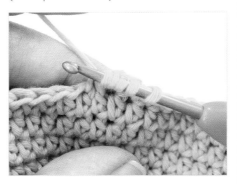

6. Yarn over and draw through 2 loops on hook (4 loops on hook).

7. Yarn over hook, insert into same stitch and pull up a loop (6 loops on hook).

8. Yarn over and draw through 2 loops on hook (5 loops on hook).

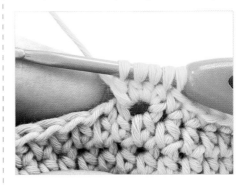

9. Yarn over hook, insert into same stitch and pull up a loop (7 loops on hook).

10. Yarn over and draw through 2 loops on hook (6 loops on hook).

11. Yarn over and draw through remaining 6 loops on hook.

12. Chain 1 to secure.

Note: *For the Small Bobble, repeat steps 1-8, ending with 5 loops on hook. Yarn over and draw through remaining 5 loops on hook, and chain 1 to secure and complete Small Bobble.*

SPECIAL EMBROIDERY STITCHES

French Knot

This is a decorative embroidery stitch that I like using to create "dots" on a crochet piece, either for buttons or an animal nose.

1. Thread a strand of yarn through needle. Enter the crochet piece from the back to the front. Pull the yarn and needle out some ways from the piece. Wrap the working tail around the needle 3 or 4 times (depending on how thick you want your dot to be).

2. Push the loops together and while holding them in place, pass the needle through these loops and pull tight. A bump will form on your yarn strand.

3. Insert needle in the next stitch from front to back, making sure the knot stays on the front. At the back, tie the ends in a knot to secure.

Back Stitch

Bring threaded needle up from wrong to right side of your amigurumi (#1). Insert needle back down (#2) and out again (#3). Then insert in same place where you came out (#1). Repeat according to the length required.

Straight Stitch

Bring threaded needle up from wrong to right side of your amigurumi, at the position you want to start the stitch (#1). Insert the needle back into the amigurumi at the position you want to end the stitch (#2). You may go over the same two positions several times to make a thicker straight stitch.

TIPS & TECHNIQUES

Double Magic Ring

The Double Magic Ring is a great technique to master. Whenever I crochet in rounds, I always start with a double magic ring as it leaves only a tiny gap once the ring is pulled closed.

A normal magic ring can also be used, but remember to secure the ring and weave in the tail after you have worked a few rounds.

1. Wrap the yarn tail twice around your finger.

2. Insert the hook under the two loops and pull the working yarn through. Do not tighten up the ring.

3. Wrap the working yarn over the hook and draw the yarn through the loop on the hook. This secures the ring and does not count as a stitch.

4. Work the required stitches in Round 1 over both the loops into the ring.

5. When all the stitches are done, gently tug one of the loops (that formed the double loop on your finger) to close the ring.

6. Then tug on tail to tighten up the remaining loose loop. Round 1 worked in a Magic Ring is complete.

Working Around a Foundation Chain

This is ideal for making an oval piece I use it in the patterns throughout this book to make the shoes for each doll.

1. Chain the required amount of stitches called for in the pattern.

2. Starting in the second chain from the hook, work single crochet stitches in each chain across, but stop before working the last chain.

3. In the last chain, you make three single crochet stitches all in the same chain stitch, so that you end up on the other side of the foundation chain - instead of "turning" your work, you will be "rotating" to the other side.

4. Now you'll be working single crochet stitches in the other loops of the foundation chain across to the end. This will form the base - or Round 1 - of your oval piece.

Changing Colors

When the pattern calls for a color change, you need to start changing colors in the stitch right before - the new color needs to be picked up in the final step before you complete the last stitch of the current color.

1. When you reach the last stitch before changing colors - make the stitch as you normally would until you have two loops remaining on the hook.

2. This is where you will pick up the new color and pull it through the remaining loops on the hook.

3. You can then continue crocheting in the new color.

Managing Yarn Tails in Color Changes

There are several ways to manage the yarn tail (of the old color) when you make a color change.

a) Cut and Tie Method

When you no longer need to go back to the old color, you can cut the old color and tie the old and new color tails together on the inside of your amigurumi piece.

b) Drop and Pick-up Method

When a pattern calls for alternating between colors at each round, and the color change happens at the start of every round, you don't have to cut the yarn of the previous color.

Just drop the old color to the inside of the work and then pick it up again when it is needed.

This will create a strand on the inside. Keep the strands slightly loose so the crochet piece does not pucker.

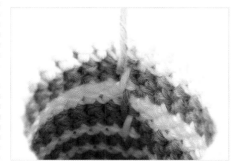

c) Carry-Along Method

This technique is very useful in patterns where a color change is used to create a special design on a piece.

Instead of cutting or dropping the yarn, you will "carry" the yarn along on the inside of the amigurumi piece (holding it together with the working yarn), as you make each stitch with the new color.

When it's time to change back to the old color, simply switch to the old color (which will now be the new color), and carry along the yarn from the previous color instead. You can do this back and forth until the color change is no longer needed.

Note: You may have to tug to tighten the yarn that is carried along frequently to make sure that the color doesn't show through on the right side of your amigurumi.

Fasten Off

At the end of your crochet work, you need to fasten off to ensure that your yarn does not unravel.

1. After the last stitch is made, cut the yarn, leaving a tail.

2. Yarn over hook and pull the yarn tail through the stitch. Tug to secure. This is how you "fasten off".

3. Keep the tail long for pieces that require sewing.

Needle Join
(also known as Invisible Join)

This technique gives a clean finish to your pieces.

1. After the last stitch is made, cut the yarn and pull the tail through the stitch.

2. Thread the tail onto a yarn needle. Skip the next stitch and insert the needle under both loops of the following stitch. Pull yarn through.

3. Then insert the needle into the back loop of the last stitch made (the same stitch where the tail came through).

4. Pull the yarn gently so that it looks like a stitch and matches the size of the other stitches.

Close the Remaining Stitches

You can close the small hole made in the last round by using this method:

1. After fastening off, thread the yarn tail onto a needle.

2. Working in the last round of stitches, insert the needle in and out of all the front loops of each stitch around.

3. Pull the tail gently to close the center hole completely.

4. Usually at this point you secure with a knot or double stitch – before hiding the tail.

5. Insert needle back through the center hole into the stuffed piece and bring it back out on another side of your amigurumi.

6. Holding the tail taut, trim excess yarn.

7. The tail should disappear inside your piece.

Weave in Ends

When the yarn tail is no longer needed, you will need to "weave in ends".

1. Thread the yarn tail onto a needle.

2. Starting close to where the tail begins, working on the wrong side of your work, weave the tail through the back of the stitches.

3. Thread remaining tail ends inside your amigurumi to hide them. You can make a knot to ensure that they do not unravel. Trim excess.

Sewing Pieces Together

This step is usually the last step before completing your amigurumi, and one wrong move could ruin everything! Some things to remember:

1. A good habit to have is to pin the pieces in place first to check on their positions.

2. Make sure all the parts are facing the right way (head and limbs).

3. Hide unsightly jagged striped lines at the back, or on the underside of an arm.

a) Whipstitch

I use this stitch throughout, mostly to attach a "closed" piece to another "closed" piece (like an arm that is pinched close, attached onto the body).

1. With both pieces right-side facing, insert your needle through a crocheted stitch on the first piece, from front to back.

2. Bring the needle up through the corresponding stitch on the second piece, from back to front.

3. Insert your needle in the next stitch on the first piece from front to back. Repeat Steps 1 & 2.

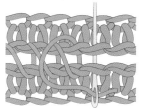

Mattress Stitch

This stitch creates an almost invisible seam when done neatly. I use this for attaching an "open" piece to a "closed" piece.

1. On the first piece, insert your needle in the same place where it came out and bring it up under the next stitch.

2. On the second piece, insert your needle in the same place where it came out and bring it up under the next stitch.

3. Repeat steps 1 & 2.

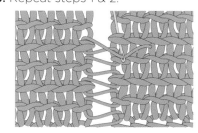

Stuffing Pieces

When it comes to stuffing your amigurumi, the more you stuff, the better your piece will hold its shape. Even a small tiny amigurumi may need quite a lot of stuffing, especially main body parts or legs which help a doll stand.

So, how do you know how much stuffing to use? Your doll should feel firm to the touch and not overly-squishy. But be careful not to over-stuff. You will know this has happened when you start to see stuffing peeking through your stitches.

When crocheting a piece that starts out with a smaller section (like a pair of legs that flows into the body), remember to start stuffing as you go along, or you may end up having a hard time trying to reach all the way into the amigurumi to fill all the parts up firmly. I like to use the back of my Clover Amour Hooks to push the stuffing in.

Using Safety Eyes & Scrapbooking Brads

You can change the look of your amigurumi entirely just by using smaller or bigger safety eyes. In this book we are using oval-shaped safety eyes, but feel free to switch them to circular ones. Adding "eye whites" to the side of your safety eyes will give your dolls a curious expression. You can do so either by making several straight stitches using white yarn or glue on a small piece of white felt cut out in a half-moon shape.

I also like using colored scrapbooking brads to add detail to the face. Throughout the book, I have used orange brads for the "nose".

When making toys for babies and young children, please consider embroidering the eyes and nose using either yarn or embroidery floss.

Surface Single Crochet

I use this often to add dimension to an amigurumi piece, usually for cuffs on pants and sleeves.

I also use it to make a foundation round when I need to crochet a piece of clothing that flows independently from the doll's body, like a skirt or a cardigan.

1. To start, make a slip knot on your hook. Insert hook into a stitch on your amigurumi piece from the front (right side) and out to a stitch next to it.

2. Yarn over and pull through both stitch holes. Now you will have 2 loops on the hook.

3. Yarn over and pull through both loops on the hook. Your first surface single crochet is made.

4. To make the next stitch, insert hook in the current stitch and out in the next stitch. Repeat instructions 2 and 3 above, until you have the number of stitches required.

Working in Front and Back Loops Only

Looking at crochet stitches, you can see a row of ">"s along the top. These are made up of **front** and **back loops**.

Unless otherwise instructed, all stitches are worked under both loops.

The front loop is the loop closest to you and the back loop is the loop furthest from you.

Working in **back loops** only creates a raised ridge on your piece.

This can be left alone for decorative purposes, or it can be used when working in the "unused front loops", which is useful for attaching on a new layer of work, for instance a skirt or a sleeve cuff.

Adding a Layer of Clothing

As they say, nice clothes can add to a personality. Each and every doll in this book has a unique sense of fashion. Some articles of clothing are removable, while others are worked directly onto the Body.

When crocheting directly onto the Doll, there are two ways you can try:

a) Working Round 1 with Surface Single Crochet

Using the Surface Single Crochet technique, work Round 1 directly onto the Body of the Doll.

1. Turn the Body of the Doll upside down. With a slipknot on your hook, make the first surface single crochet into any stitch (or as indicated) on the last round of the Body.

2. Continue to crochet all around. If you are making a skirt or a shirt, you will join the round with a slip stitch to the first stitch. If it's a coat or a cardigan, you will stop at the last stitch, make a chain and turn your work.

3. You can then continue on with the rest of the rounds, using Round 1 as your foundation round to build an independent layer of clothing from the Body.

b) Working Directly onto Unused Front Loops

Whenever you crochet in the **back loops** only, you create a series of unused front loops. These can be left alone as a decorative design. I like putting them to a better use by crocheting directly onto these front loops, usually to make a flowing skirt for the Doll.

1. Turn the Body of the Doll upside down. With a slipknot on your hook, make the first single crochet into any stitch (or as indicated) on the unused front loops on the Body.

2. Single crochet all around Body. Join the round with a slip stitch.

3. Continue with the rest of the rounds as instructed.

PROJECTS

Sleepy-Time
Sophie

There may be bedtime battles with other kids, but not with little Sophie.
When it's time to say "Night, night!", this tiny three-year old is all smiles and
readily climbs into bed with her favorite bunny lovey.

MATERIALS & TOOLS

HELLO Cotton Yarn

» **Main Color (MC):** Powder Peach (163) - for Head, Body, Arms & Legs
» **Color A:** White (154) - for Eye Whites
» **Color B:** Salmon (109) - for Cheeks
» **Color C:** Lavender (140) - for Hair & Pigtails
» **Color D:** Mint Green (138) - for Dress & Body
» **Color E:** Light Pink (102) - for Shoes and Eye Mask
» **Color F:** Off-White (155) - for Dress Edging & Bunny
» **Color G:** Robin's Egg Blue (151) - for Eye Mask Design
» **Color H:** Light Yellow (122) - for Ribbon

Hook Sizes

» 3mm hook
» 3.5mm hook – for Hair

Other

» Stitch markers
» Yarn needle
» Stuffing
» Craft Glue
» Pins
» Safety Eyes - Black Oval 3/8" (10mm) x 2
» Scrapbooking Brad - Orange 5/32" (4mm) x 1 - for Nose
» DMC Embroidery Floss - Black
» Embroidery Needle
» Brown sewing thread & sewing needle

FINISHED SIZE	**SKILL LEVEL**
About 7" (18cm) tall	Intermediate

PATTERN NOTES

The smaller size hook is used throughout, unless otherwise stated.

SPECIAL STITCHES

Bobble (bob) (refer to Special Crochet Stitches): Yarn over, insert hook in stitch or space specified and pull up a loop (3 loops on hook), yarn over and draw through 2 loops on hook (2 loops remain); *yarn over and insert hook in same stitch or space and pull up a loop, yarn over and draw through two loops on hook; repeat from * 3 times more (6 loops on hook), yarn over and draw through all 6 loops; ch 1 to secure.

Note: The ch-1 does not count as a stitch and is skipped when working the next round.

SOPHIE

HEAD

Round 1: With MC, make a magic ring, 6 sc in ring. (6 sc)

Round 2: Inc in each st around. (12 sc)

Round 3: [Sc in next st, inc in next st] 6 times. (18 sc)

Round 4: [Sc in next 2 sts, inc in next st] 6 times. (24 sc)

Round 5: [Sc in next 3 sts, inc in next st] 6 times. (30 sc)

Round 6: [Sc in next 4 sts, inc in next st] 6 times. (36 sc)

Round 7: [Sc in next 5 sts, inc in next st] 6 times. (42 sc)

Round 8: [Sc in next 6 sts, inc in next st] 6 times. (48 sc)

Round 9: [Sc in next 7 sts, inc in next st] 6 times. (54 sc)

Round 10: [Sc in next 8 sts, inc in next st] 6 times. (60 sc)

Rounds 11-21: (11 rounds) Sc in each st around. (60 sc)

Round 22: [Sc in next 8 sts, inv-dec] 6 times. (54 sc) *(image 1)*

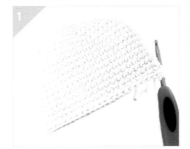

Round 23: [Sc in next 7 sts, inv-dec] 6 times. (48 sc)

Round 24: [Sc in next 6 sts, inv-dec] 6 times. (42 sc)

Add Facial Features:

1. Nose - position brad at front of Head (about 27th stitch on Round 20) and lock in place. *(image 2 & 3)*

2. Eyes - position on Round 19, about 6 stitches from either side of Nose and secure in place. *(image 4 & 5)*

3. Eye Whites - using Color A and yarn needle, make 3-4 vertical straight stitches (the same height as Eyes) to the left of each Eye. Knot and secure the yarn on the inside of the Head. *(image 6)*

Continue crocheting:

Round 25: [Sc in next 5 sts, inv-dec] 6 times. (36 sc)

Round 26: [Sc in next 4 sts, inv-dec] 6 times. (30 sc)

Round 27: [Sc in next 3 sts, inv-dec] 6 times. (24 sc)

Start stuffing Head, adding more as you go.

Round 28: [Sc in next 2 sts, inv-dec] 6 times. (18 sc)

Round 29: [Sc in next st, inv-dec] 6 times. (12 sc)

Round 30: [Inv dec] 6 times. (6 sc) Fasten off.

Close the opening securely and leave a long tail (for Eye Indentations). *(image 7)*

Cheek (Make 2)

Round 1: With Color B, make a magic ring, 6 sc in ring. (6 sc)

Fasten off with Needle Join, leaving a long tail for sewing.

FINISHING THE FACE

Eye Indentations

Using long tail on Head and yarn needle:

1. Bring needle up from base of Head and out next to the nose-side of Eye. *(image 8)*

2. Insert needle in next stitch, bringing it out at base of Head. Gently tug yarn to create a slight indentation at the Eye. *(image 9)*

3. Repeat steps 1 & 2 for other Eye. *(image 10 & 11)*

4. Secure yarn tail with a knot at base of Head and trim excess yarn.

Cheeks - Position the Cheeks below each Eye and sew in place, bringing the yarn out at base of Head. Secure with a knot and trim excess yarn. *(image 12)*

Eyebrows & Mouth

Using Black Embroidery Floss and needle:

1. Bring needle up from base of Head and embroider Eyebrows above each Eye – by making a diagonal straight stitch from Round 16 to Round 17, about 4 stitches long. *(image 13)*

2. After Eyebrows, bring needle down through Head to create a Mouth on Round 22, centered under the Nose – by making a loose horizontal straight stitch, about 3 stitches long, bringing needle out at base of Head. Tie ends in a knot to secure and trim excess yarn. *(image 14)*

3. Optional: Apply glue on Mouth, and use pins to shape the smile while the glue dries. *(image 15 & 16)*

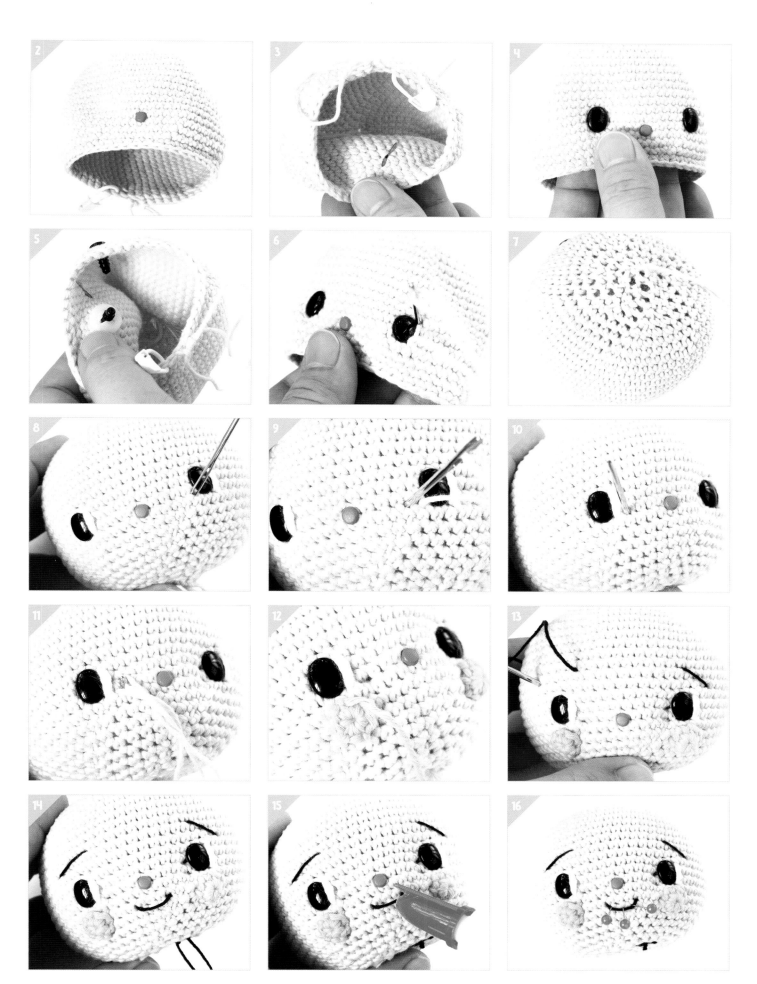

HAIR

Rounds 1-10: With Color C and larger hook, repeat Rounds 1-10 of Head.

Rounds 11-13: (3 rounds) Sc in each st around. (60 sc)

Work continues in Rows

Row 1: (Wrong Side) Ch 1, turn, sc in next 38 sts. (38 sc) Leave remaining sts unworked.

Rows 2-6 (5 rows): Ch 1, turn, sc in each st across. (38 sc) *(image 17)*

The final round is worked all around the Hair to neaten the edges.

Last Round: Ch 1, turn, (wrong side facing) sc in first st, sc in next 36 sts, 2 sc in last st; working in sides of rows, sc in each of next 5 rows; working across bangs, sc in next 23 sts; working in sides of rows, sc in each of next 5 rows, sc in same st as first st. (72 sc)

Fasten off, leaving a long tail for sewing.

Pigtail (Make 4)

Row 1: With Color C and smaller hook, ch 25, starting in 2nd ch from hook, dc in each ch across. (24 dc)

Fasten off, leaving a long tail for sewing. *(image 18)*

Twist 2 pieces together in a spiral, then fold everything in half to meet the starting edge. Make a few stitches to secure this shape. *(image 19 & 20)*

Repeat on the other 2 pieces to make another pigtail.

Attaching Hair

1. Position the Hair on the Head and sew in place using backstitches. *(image 21)*

2. Sew the Pigtails to each side of the Hair/Head. *(image 22)*

BODY

Rounds 1-5: Using Color D, repeat Rounds 1-5 of Head.

Rounds 6-9: (4 rounds) Sc in each st around. (30 sc)

Change to MC.

Rounds 10-17: (8 rounds) Sc in each st around. (30 sc)

Round 18: [Sc in next 3 sts, inv-dec] 6 times. (24 sc)

Fasten off, leaving a long tail for sewing.

Stuff Body firmly. *(image 23)*

ARM (Make 2)

Round 1: With MC, make a magic ring, 6 sc in ring. (6 sc)

Round 2: Inc in each st around. (12 sc)

Rounds 3-4: (2 rounds) Sc in each st around. (12 sc)

Round 5: [Inv-dec] 3 times, sc in next 6 sts. (9 sc)

Rounds 6-13: (8 rounds) Sc in each st around. (9 sc)

Fasten off, leaving a long tail for sewing.

Stuff Arm lightly. *(image 24)*

LEG - with Shoe (Make 2)

Round 1: With Color E, ch 8; starting in 2nd ch from hook, sc in next 6 ch, 3 sc in last ch; working on other side of starting chain, sc in next 6 ch. (15 sc) *(image 25 & 26)*

Round 2: Inc in first st, sc in next 6 sts, inc in next 2 sts, sc in next 5 sts, inc in last st. (19 sc) *(image 27)*

Round 3: Working in **back loops** only, sc in each st around. (19 sc) *(image 28)*

Round 4: Working in both loops, sc in each st around. (19 sc) *(image 29)*

Change to MC.

Round 5: Working in **back loops** only, sc in next 8 sts, [inv-dec] 3 times, sc in next 5 sts. (16 sc) *(image 30)*

At the end of Round 5, cut Color E and tie it together with the tail of MC. Trim the tails. *(image 31)*

Round 6: Working in both loops, sc in next 7 sts, [inv-dec] 4 times, sc in last st. (12 sc)

Rounds 7-13: (7 rounds) Sc in each st around. (12 sc)

Fasten off, leaving a long tail for sewing.

Stuff legs firmly. *(image 32)*

Bunny Ears for Shoe (Make 2)

With Color E, ch 6, sc in 2nd ch from hook, sc in each of next 3 ch, (sc, sl st) in last ch *(first ear made)*; ch 6, sc in 2nd ch from hook, sc in each next 4 ch. *(second ear made)*.

Fasten off, leaving a long tail for sewing.

Finishing the Shoes

Sew the Bunny Ears to the front of each Shoe on Round 4. *(image 33)*

DRESS

Row 1: With Color D, ch 40, starting in 2nd ch from hook, sc in each ch across. (39 sc)

Row 2: Ch 1, turn, working in **back loops** only, hdc in first st, hdc in next 5 sts, 2 hdc in next st, [hdc in next 6 sts, 2 hdc in next st] 4 times, hdc in next 4 sts. (44 hdc)

Row 3: Ch 1, turn, working in **front loops** only, hdc in first st, hdc in next 6 sts, 2 hdc in next st, [hdc in next 7 sts, 2 hdc] 4 times, hdc in next 4 sts. (49 hdc) *(image 34)*

Work continues in Rounds.

Round 4: *(Armholes)* Ch 1, turn, working in **back loops** only, hdc in first st, hdc in next 4 sts, ch 3, skip next 9 sts, sl st in next st, hdc in next 19 sts, ch 3, skip next 9 sts, sl st in next st, hdc in next 5 sts; join with sl st to the first st. (29 hdc, 2 sl sts & 2 ch-3 lps) *(image 35, 36 & 37)*

Round 5: Ch 1 *(do not turn)*, starting in same st as joining, sc in each st and ch around; join with sl st to first sc. (37 sc)

Round 6: Ch 1, hdc in same st as joining, 2 hdc in next st, [hdc in next st, 2 hdc in next st] 17 times, hdc in last st; join with sl st to first hdc. (55 hdc)

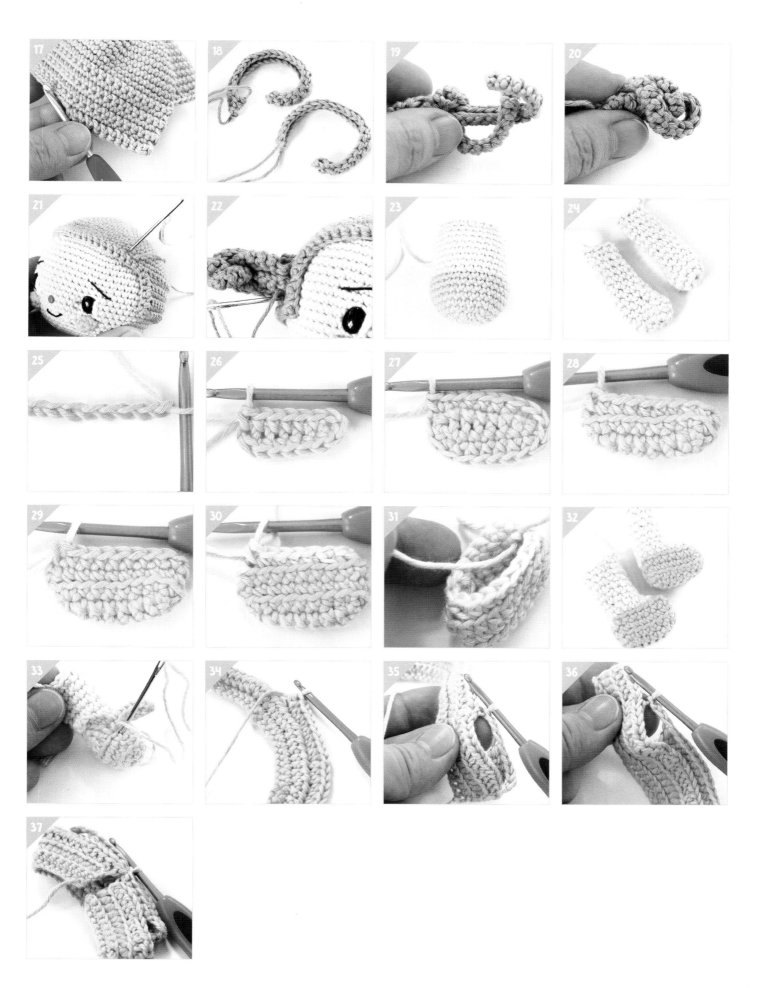

Rounds 7-9: *(3 rounds)* Ch 1, hdc in each st around; join with sl st to first hdc. (55 hdc) Change to Color F.

Round 10: *(Lace Edging)* Ch 1, hdc in first st, hdc in next 2 sts, bob in next st, sl st in next st, [hdc in next 3 sts, bob in next st, sl st in next st] 10 times; join with sl st to first hdc. (33 hdc, 11 bobble sts & 11 sl sts) *(image 38)*

Fasten off and weave in ends.

Ribbon

Row 1: With Color H, ch 30.

Fasten off, and trim tails.

Attaching Ribbon onto Dress

Loop the strand into a ribbon shape.

Thread a strand of Color H onto a needle and sew the Ribbon to the front of the Dress, making several loops over the center of the Ribbon. *(image 39)*

EYE MASK

Round 1: With Color E, ch 16; starting in 2nd ch from hook, sc in next 14 ch, 3 sc in last ch, working on other side of starting chain, sc in next 13 ch, inc in the last ch. (32 sc)

Round 2: Inc in first st, sc in next 14 sts, 3 sc in next st, sc in next 15 sts, inc in the last st. (36 sc)

Round 3: Inc in first st, sc in next 16 sts, 3 sc in next st, sc in next 17 sts, inc in the last st. (40 sc)

Round 4: 2 hdc in first st, hdc in next 8 sts, sl st in next 2 sts, hdc in next 8 sts, 2 hdc in next st, sc in next 20 sts. (20 hdc, 20 sc & 2 sl sts)

Last Row: Sc in next 10 sts, sl st in next 3 sts, sc in next 6 sts, inc in next 3 sts, sc in next 3 sts. (25 sts & 3 sl sts) Leave remaining sts unworked.

Fasten off and weave in ends.

Eye Mask Detail

Using Color G and a yarn needle, embroider "closed eyelids with eyelashes" design on front of Eye Mask. *(image 40)*

BUNNY TOY

Round 1: With Color F, make a magic ring, 6 sc in ring. (6 sc)

Round 2: Inc in each st around. (12 sc)

Round 3: [Sc in next 3 sts, inc in next st] 3 times. (15 sc)

Rounds 4-6: *(3 rounds)* Sc in each st around. (15 sc)

Round 7: Sc in next 5 sts, bob in next st, sl st in next st, sc in next 2 sts, bob in next st, sl st in next st, sc in next 4 sts. (11 sc, 2 bobble sts & 2 sl sts)

Round 8: Sc in each st around. (15 sc)

Round 9: Sc in next 6 sts, bob in next st, sl st in next st, sc in next 2 sts, bob in next st, sl st in next st, sc in next 3 sts. (11 sc, 2 bobble sts & 2 sl sts)

Round 10: Sc in each st around. (15 sc)

Round 11: [Sc in next 3 sts, inv-dec] 3 times. (12 sc)

Start stuffing the bunny.

Round 12: [Inv-dec] 6 times. (6 sc)

Finish stuffing and close the opening securely, leaving a long tail for sewing.

Bunny Ears for Toy

Using Color F, repeat instructions of Bunny Ears for Shoes.

Bunny Toy Assembly

• Sew Bunny Ears to head of Bunny Toy.

• With brown sewing thread, embroider a face on Bunny.

• Using Color B, embroider several backstitches for Cheeks. *(image 41)*

FINAL DOLL ASSEMBLY

1. Sew Body to finished Head, adding more stuffing before finishing. *(image 42)*

2. Position Legs and sew in place, adding more stuffing so Doll can stand when propped up against a wall. *(image 43)*

3. Position Arms and sew in place. *(image 44)*

4. Slip Dress over Doll. *(image 45)*

5. Position Eye Mask on top of Head. Using strand of Color G, make a band to loop around Head/Hair to hold the Eye Mask in place. Several small stitches can be sewn (using Color E) to secure the Eye Mask to the Head/Hair, *(image 46)*

6. Sew Bunny Toy to one Arm.

Helena

The Doctor

Dr Helena is the friendliest doctor in town, and all the children love her so.
Her clinic is packed full of stuffed toys, stickers and children's books.
Indeed, her little patients never leave with any tears in their eyes, even if they
have a Band-Aid on a finger or a bandage on a knee!

MATERIALS & TOOLS

HELLO Cotton Yarn

» **Main Color (MC):** Powder Peach (163) - for Head, Body & Arms
» **Color A:** White (154) - for Eye Whites
» **Color B:** Light Pink (102) - for Cheeks
» **Color C:** Baby Pink (101) - for Hair
» **Color D:** Turquoise (134) - for Shirt, Arms & Legs
» **Color E:** Off-White (155) - for Coat & Shoes
» **Color F:** Cherry Red (113) - for Shoe Detail
» **Color G:** Light Grey (175) - for Stethoscope
» **Color H:** Sky Blue (147) - for Stethoscope

Hook Sizes

» 3mm hook

Other

» Stitch markers
» Yarn needle
» Stuffing
» Craft Glue
» Pins
» Safety Eyes - Black Oval 3/8" (10mm) x 2
» Scrapbooking Brad - Orange 5/32" (4mm) x 1 - for Nose
» DMC Embroidery Floss - Black
» Embroidery Needle
» Jewelry wire – 4⅔" (12cm) long for Stethoscope
» Wire cutter

FINISHED SIZE
About 7¼" (18.5cm) tall

SKILL LEVEL
Intermediate

PATTERN NOTES

When working double crochet rounds, the first ch-2 does not count as the first stitch. The first dc of the round is worked in the same stitch as the previous round's join.

SPECIAL STITCHES

Surface Single Crochet (refer to Tips & Techniques): With right side of crochet piece facing, work between the stitches. Start with a slip knot on the hook and insert it in specified stitch and out in next stitch; pull up a loop (2 loops on hook); yarn over hook and draw through both loops on hook. (Standing surface single crochet made)

For following stitches, insert hook in stitch where the hook came out of and out again in next stitch; pull up a loop (2 loops on hook); yarn over and draw through both loops. (Surface single crochet made)

HELENA

HEAD

Round 1: With MC, make a magic ring, 6 sc in ring. (6 sc)

Round 2: Inc in each st around. (12 sc)

Round 3: [Sc in next st, inc in next st] 6 times. (18 sc)

Round 4: [Sc in next 2 sts, inc in next st] 6 times. (24 sc)

Round 5: [Sc in next 3 sts, inc in next st] 6 times. (30 sc)

Round 6: [Sc in next 4 sts, inc in next st] 6 times. (36 sc)

Round 7: [Sc in next 5 sts, inc in next st] 6 times. (42 sc)

Round 8: [Sc in next 6 sts, inc in next st] 6 times. (48 sc)

Round 9: [Sc in next 7 sts, inc in next st] 6 times. (54 sc)

Round 10: [Sc in next 8 sts, inc in next st] 6 times. (60 sc)

Rounds 11-21: (11 rounds) Sc in each st around. (60 sc)

Round 22: [Sc in next 8 sts, inv-dec] 6 times. (54 sc) *(image 1)*

Round 23: [Sc in next 7 sts, inv-dec] 6 times. (48 sc)

Round 24: [Sc in next 6 sts, inv-dec] 6 times. (42 sc)

Add Facial Features:

1. Nose - position brad at front of Head (about 27th stitch on Round 20) and lock in place. *(image 2 & 3)*

2. Eyes - position on Round 19, about 6 stitches from either side of Nose and secure in place. *(image 4 & 5)*

3. Eye Whites - using Color A and yarn needle, make 3-4 vertical straight stitches (the same height as Eyes) to the left of each Eye. Knot and secure the yarn on the inside of the Head. *(image 6)*

Continue Crocheting:

Round 25: [Sc in next 5 sts, inv-dec] 6 times. (36 sc)

Round 26: [Sc in next 4 sts, inv-dec] 6 times. (30 sc)

Round 27: [Sc in next 3 sts, inv-dec] 6 times. (24 sc)

Start stuffing Head, adding more as you go.

Round 28: [Sc in next 2 sts, inv-dec] 6 times. (18 sc)

Round 29: [Sc in next st, inv-dec] 6 times. (12 sc)

Round 30: [Inv dec] 6 times. (6 sc) Fasten off.
Close the opening securely and leave a long tail (for Eye Indentations). *(image 7)*

Cheek (Make 2)

Round 1: With Color B, make a magic ring, 6 sc in ring. (6 sc)

Fasten off with Needle Join, leaving a long tail for sewing.

FINISHING THE FACE

Eye Indentations

Using long tail on Head and yarn needle:

1. Bring needle up from base of Head and out next to the nose-side of Eye. *(image 8)*

2. Insert needle in next stitch, bringing it out at base of Head. Gently tug yarn to create a slight indentation at the Eye. *(image 9)*

3. Repeat steps 1 & 2 for other Eye. *(image 10 & 11)*

4. Secure yarn tail with a knot at base of Head and trim excess yarn.

Cheeks - Position the Cheeks below each Eye and sew in place, bringing the yarn out at base of Head. Secure with a knot and trim excess yarn. *(image 12)*

Eyebrows & Mouth

Using Black Embroidery Floss and needle:

1. Bring needle up from base of Head and embroider Eyebrows above each Eye – by making a diagonal straight stitch from Round 16 to Round 17, about 4 stitches long. *(image 13)*

2. After Eyebrows, bring needle down through Head to create a Mouth on Round 22, centered under the Nose – by making a loose horizontal straight stitch, about 4 stitches long, bringing needle out at base of Head. Tie ends in a knot to secure and trim excess yarn. *(image 14)*

3. Optional: Apply glue on Mouth, and use pins to shape the smile while the glue dries. *(image 15 & 16)*

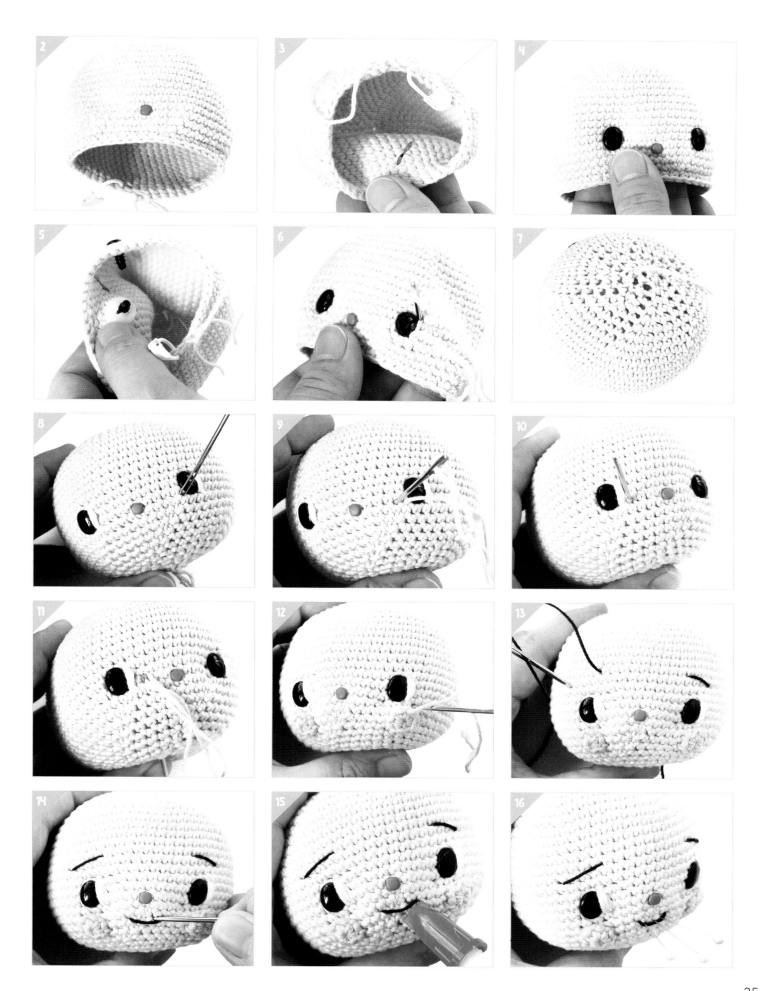

HAIR

Large Hair Piece – Make 1

Round 1: With Color C, make a magic ring, ch 2 (does not count as first st), 10 dc in ring; join with sl st to first dc. (10 dc)

Round 2: Ch 2, 2 dc in each st around; join with sl st to first dc. (20 dc)

Round 3: Ch 2, [dc in next st, 2 dc in next st] 10 times; join with sl st to first dc. (30 dc)

Rounds 4-14: *(11 rounds)* Ch 2, dc in each st around; join with sl st to first dc. (30 dc)

Fasten off, leaving a long tail for sewing.

Do not stuff. Flatten piece.

Small Hair Piece - Make 5

Round 1: With Color C, make a magic ring, ch 2 (does not count as first st), 10 dc in ring; join with sl st to first dc. (10 dc)

Round 2: Ch 2, 2 dc in each st around; join with sl st to first dc. (20 dc)

Rounds 3-11: *(9 rounds)* Ch 2, dc in each st around; join with sl st to first dc. (20 dc)

Fasten off, leaving a long tail for sewing.

Do not stuff. Flatten piece. *(image 17)*

Attaching Hair

1. Arrange the Small Hair Pieces around the sides and back of Head, leaving the face uncovered. *(image 18)*

2. Position the Large Hair Piece to cover the crown, and overlapping the smaller pieces on one side. *(image 19 & 20)*

3. Sew all Hair Pieces in place with backstitches around top of pieces. *(image 21)*

4. Secure the pieces by sewing on the underside of them to keep the stitches hidden. *(image 22 & 23)*

BODY

Round 1: Using Color D, make a magic ring, 6 sc in ring. (6 sc)

Round 2: Inc in each st around. (12 sc)

Round 3: [Sc in next st, inc in next st] 6 times. (18 sc)

Round 4: [Sc in next 2 sts, inc in next st] 6 times. (24 sc)

Round 5: [Sc in next 3 sts, inc in next st] 6 times. (30 sc)

Rounds 6-10: *(5 rounds)* Sc in each st around. (30 sc)
Change to MC.

Rounds 11-18: *(8 rounds)* Sc in each st around. (30 sc)

Round 19: [Sc in next 3 sts, inv-dec] 6 times. (24 sc)
Move marker to 7th stitch – for Shirt joining.

Fasten off, leaving a long tail for sewing.

Stuff body firmly.

SHIRT

Note: *Round 1 is worked around Round 19 of Body using Surface Single Crochet.*

Round 1: Holding the Body upside down, join Color D with a standing sc to marked st on Round 19, sc in next 24 sts, ch 8, join with sl st to first sc. (25 sc & ch-8) *(image 24)*

Round 2: Ch 1, hdc in same st as joining, hdc in next 2 sts, 2 hdc in the next st, [hdc in next 3 sts, 2 hdc in next st] 5 times, working in ch-8, hdc in next 8 ch; join with sl st to first hdc. (38 hdc) *(image 25)*

Rounds 3-8: *(6 rounds)* Ch 1, hdc in each st around; join with sl st to first hdc. (38 hdc) *(image 26)*

Round 9: Ch 1, working in **back loops** only, sc in each st around; join with sl st to first sc. (38 sc)

Fasten off and weave in ends.

ARM (Make 2)

Round 1: With MC, make a magic ring, 6 sc in ring. (6 sc)

Round 2: Inc in each st around. (12 sc)

Rounds 3-4: *(2 rounds)* Sc in each st around. (12 sc)

Round 5: [Inv-dec] 3 times, sc in next 6 sts. (9 sc)

Rounds 6-11: *(6 rounds)* Sc in each st around. (9 sc)
Change to Color D.

Rounds 12-13: *(2 rounds)* Sc in each st around. (9 sc)

Fasten off, leaving a long tail for sewing.

Stuff arm lightly. *(image 27)*

COAT

Row 1: With Color E, ch 37, starting in 2nd ch from hook, hdc in each ch across. (36 hdc)

Row 2: Ch 1, turn, 2 hdc in first st, hdc in next 5 sts, [2 hdc in next st, hdc in next 5 sts] across. (42 hdc).

Row 3: Ch 1, turn, 2 hdc in first st, hdc in next 6 sts, [2 hdc in next st, hdc in next 6 sts] across. (48 hdc).

Row 4: (Armholes) Ch 1, turn, hdc in first st, hdc in next 7 sts, ch 6, skip next 6 sts, sc in next st, hdc in next 18 sts, ch 6, skip next 6 sts, sc in next st, hdc in next 8 sts. (34 hdc, 2 sc & 2 ch-6)

Row 5: Ch 1, turn, hdc in first st, hdc in next 7 sts, skip next sc, hdc in next 5 ch, skip last ch, hdc in next 18 sts, skip next sc, hdc in next 5 ch, skip last ch, hdc in next 8 sts. (44 hdc) *(image 28)*

Rows 6-7: *(2 rows)* Ch 1, turn, hdc in each st across. (44 hdc)

Row 8: Ch 1, turn, hdc in first st, hdc in next 7 sts, 2 hdc in next st, hdc in next 22 sts, 2 hdc in next st, hdc in next 12 sts. (46 hdc)

Row 9: Ch 1, turn, hdc in each st across. (46 hdc)

Row 10: Ch 1, turn, hdc in first st, hdc in next 8 sts, 2 hdc in next st, hdc in next 24 sts, 2 hdc in next st, hdc in next 11 sts. (48 hdc)

Row 11: Ch 1, turn, hdc in each st across. (48 hdc) *(image 29)*

The final round is worked all around the edges of the Coat.

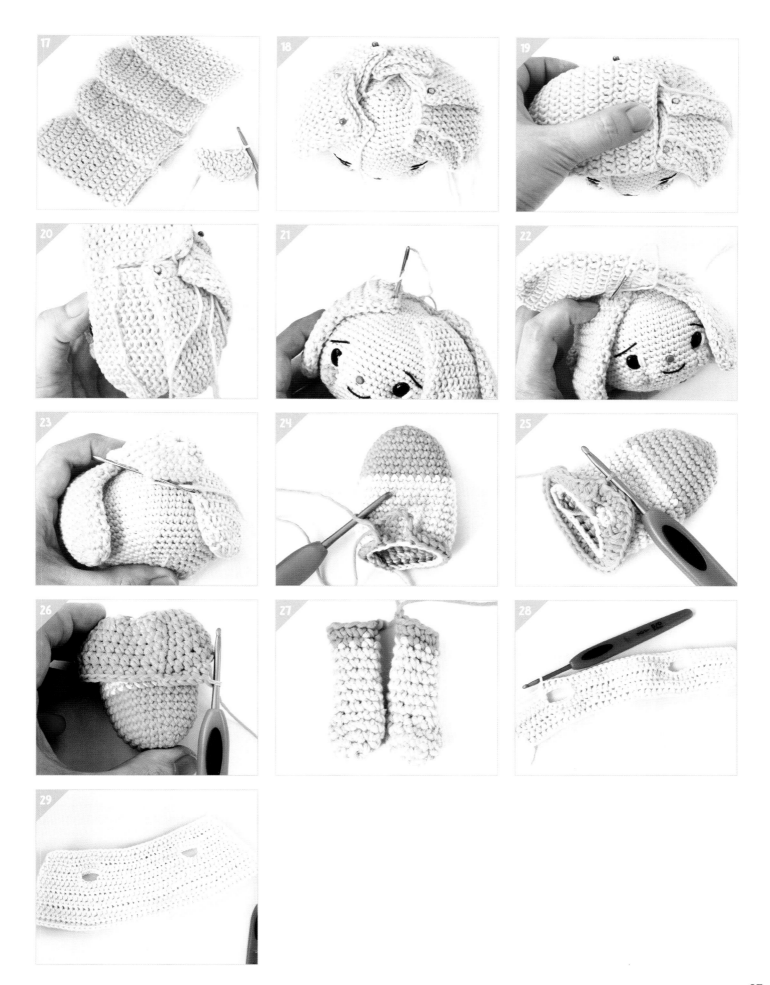

Last Round: Sc in same st as last hdc worked in Row 11; working in sides of rows, [2 sc in next row, sc in next row] 5 times; working in starting ch, 2 sc in first ch, sc in next 34 ch, 2 sc in last ch; working in sides of rows, [sc in next row, 2 sc in next row] 5 times; working in Row 11, 2 sc in first st *(image 30)*, sc in next 46 sts, 2 sc in last st. (119 sc)

Fasten off with Needle Join and weave in ends.

Coat Sleeves

The Sleeves are worked directly into the Armholes.

Round 1: With right side facing, join Color E with standing sc to any st at underarm, work 14 sc around armhole; join with sl st to first sc. (15 sc)

Rounds 2-3 *(2 rounds)*: Ch 1, hdc in each st around, sl st. (15 hdc)

Round 4: Ch 1, sc in each st around, sl st. (15 sc)

Fasten off with Needle Join and weave in ends. *(image 31)*

Repeat for other Sleeve.

LEG with Shoe (Make 2)

Round 1: With Color E, ch 8; starting in 2nd ch from hook, sc in next 6 ch, 3 sc in last ch; working on other side of starting chain, sc in next 6 ch. (15 sc)

Round 2: Inc in first st, sc in next 6 sts, inc in next 2 sts, sc in next 5 sts, inc in last st. (19 sc)

Round 3: Working in **back loops** only, sc in each st around. (19 sc)

Round 4: Working in both loops, sc in each st around. (19 sc)

Round 5: Sc in next 8 sts, [inv-dec] 3 times, sc in next 5 sts. (16 sc)

Change to Color D.

Round 6: Sc in next 7 sts, [inv-dec] 4 times, sc in last st. (12 sc)

Rounds 7-13: *(7 rounds)* Sc in each st around. (12 sc) *(image 32)*

Fasten off, leaving a long tail for sewing.

Stuff legs firmly.

STETHOSCOPE

Tubing

With Color H, make a magic ring, 8 sc in ring; join with sl st to first sc. (8 sc)

Ch 8, then fasten off, leaving a long tail for sewing.

Headset

1. Working over the jewelry wire (similar to working in a magic ring), using Color G, starting with about a 4" tail, make a standing sc over the wire, work 19 more sc over the wire. *(image 33)*
Finish off, leaving about a 4" yarn tail.

2. Trim the wire, with a short end exposed on either side of the stitches. *(image 34)*

3. Wrap each yarn tail around the ends of the wire, using glue to secure in place. *(image 35 & 36)*

4. Bend the Headset into shape. *(image 37)*

5. Sew Tubing to the center of the Headset to form the Stethoscope. *(image 38)*

FINAL DOLL ASSEMBLY

1. Sew the Body to the finished Head, adding more stuffing before finishing. *(image 39)*

2. Position the Arms and sew in place. *(image 40)*

3. Position the Legs and sew in place. Add more stuffing so your doll can stand when propped up against a wall. *(image 41)*

4. Slip Coat over doll. *(image 42)*

5. Place Stethoscope on Doll. *(image 43)*

6. Using Color F and a yarn needle, sew a strip of backstitches at the base of the Shoes. *(image 44)*

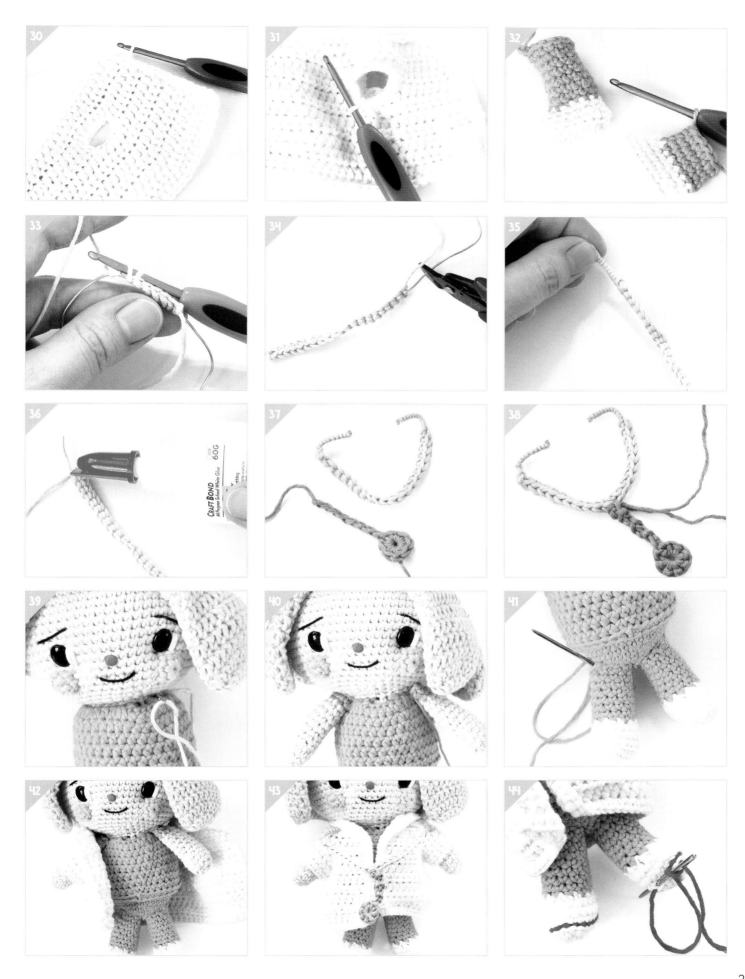

Ollie
The Firefighter

From putting out raging forest wildfires to saving a cat stuck on a roof, this courageous guy has seen it all. Ollie is a hero and is admired by all the people in town. His firetruck is his joy, and he cleans and polishes it until it shines.

MATERIALS & TOOLS

HELLO Cotton Yarn

» **Main Color (MC):** Powder Peach (163) - for Head
» **Color A:** White (154) - for Eye Whites
» **Color B:** Baby Pink (101) - for Cheeks
» **Color C:** Turquoise (134) - for Hair
» **Color D:** Yellow (123) - for Legs, Body, Arms & Badge
» **Color E:** Cherry Red (113) - for Legs, Body, Arms & Helmet
» **Color F:** Bright Orange (118) - for Shoes, Body & Badge
» **Color G:** Black (160) - for Shoes & Gloves
» **Color H:** Brown (126) - for Buttons
» **Color I:** Light Gray (175) - for Badge

Hook Sizes

» 3mm hook – Main Hook
» 3.5mm hook – for Hair
» 5mm hook – for Helmet

Other

» Stitch markers
» Yarn needle
» Stuffing
» Craft Glue
» Pins
» Safety Eyes - Black Oval 3/8" (10mm) x 2
» Scrapbooking Brad – Orange 5/32" (4mm) x 1 - for Nose
» DMC Embroidery Floss - Black
» Embroidery Needle

FINISHED SIZE	SKILL LEVEL
About 8" (20cm) tall	Intermediate

PATTERN NOTES

The main hook is used throughout, unless otherwise stated.

SPECIAL STITCHES

Surface Single Crochet (refer to Tips & Techniques) : With right side of crochet piece facing, work between the stitches. Start with a slip knot on the hook and insert it in specified stitch and out in next stitch; pull up a loop *(2 loops on hook)*; yarn over hook and draw through both loops on hook. *(Standing surface single crochet made)*

For following stitches, insert hook in stitch where the hook came out of and out again in next stitch; pull up a loop *(2 loops on hook)*; yarn over and draw through both loops. *(Surface single crochet made)*

OLLIE

HEAD

Round 1: With MC, make a magic ring, 6 sc in ring. (6 sc)

Round 2: Inc in each st around. (12 sc)

Round 3: [Sc in next st, inc in next st] 6 times. (18 sc)

Round 4: [Sc in next 2 sts, inc in next st] 6 times. (24 sc)

Round 5: [Sc in next 3 sts, inc in next st] 6 times. (30 sc)

Round 6: [Sc in next 4 sts, inc in next st] 6 times. (36 sc)

Round 7: [Sc in next 5 sts, inc in next st] 6 times. (42 sc)

Round 8: [Sc in next 6 sts, inc in next st] 6 times. (48 sc)

Round 9: [Sc in next 7 sts, inc in next st] 6 times. (54 sc)

Round 10: [Sc in next 8 sts, inc in next st] 6 times. (60 sc)

Rounds 11-21: (11 rounds) Sc in each st around. (60 sc)

Round 22: [Sc in next 8 sts, inv-dec] 6 times. (54 sc) *(image 1)*

Round 23: [Sc in next 7 sts, inv-dec] 6 times. (48 sc)

Round 24: [Sc in next 6 sts, inv-dec] 6 times. (42 sc)

Add Facial Features:

1. Nose - position brad at front of Head (about 27th stitch on Round 20) and lock in place. *(image 2 & 3)*

2. Eyes - position on Round 19, about 6 stitches from either side of Nose and secure in place. *(image 4 & 5)*

3. Eye Whites - using Color A and yarn needle, make 3-4 vertical straight stitches (the same height as Eyes) to the left of each Eye. Knot and secure the yarn on the inside of the Head. *(image 6)*

Continue crocheting:

Round 25: [Sc in next 5 sts, inv-dec] 6 times. (36 sc)

Round 26: [Sc in next 4 sts, inv-dec] 6 times. (30 sc)

Round 27: [Sc in next 3 sts, inv-dec] 6 times. (24 sc)

Start stuffing Head, adding more as you go.

Round 28: [Sc in next 2 sts, inv-dec] 6 times. (18 sc)

Round 29: [Sc in next st, inv-dec] 6 times. (12 sc)

Round 30: [Inv dec] 6 times. (6 sc) Fasten off.

Close the opening securely and leave a long tail (for Eye Indentations). *(image 7)*

Cheek (Make 2)

Round 1: With Color B, make a magic ring, 6 sc in ring. (6 sc)

Fasten off with Needle Join, leaving a long tail for sewing.

FINISHING THE FACE

Eye Indentations

Using long tail on Head and yarn needle:

1. Bring needle up from base of Head and out next to the nose-side of Eye. *(image 8)*

2. Insert needle in next stitch, bringing it out at base of Head. Gently tug yarn to create a slight indentation at the Eye. *(image 9)*

3. Repeat steps 1 & 2 for other Eye. *(image 10 & 11)*

4. Secure yarn tail with a knot at base of Head and trim excess yarn.

Cheeks - Position the Cheeks below each Eye and sew in place, bringing the yarn out at base of Head. Secure with a knot and trim excess yarn. *(image 12)*

Eyebrows & Mouth

Using Black Embroidery Floss and needle:

1. Bring needle up from base of Head and embroider Eyebrows above each Eye – by making a diagonal straight stitch from Round 16 to Round 17, about 4 stitches long. *(image 13)*

2. After Eyebrows, bring needle down through Head to create a Mouth on Round 22, centered under the Nose – by making a loose horizontal straight stitch, about 3 stitches long, bringing needle out at base of Head. Tie ends in a knot to secure and trim excess yarn. *(image 14)*

3. Optional: Apply glue on Mouth, and use pins to shape the smile while the glue dries. *(image 15 & 16)*

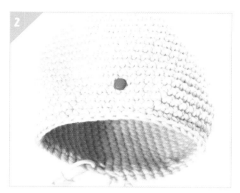

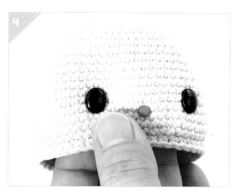

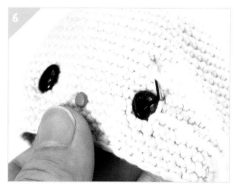
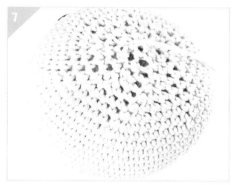

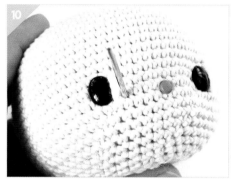

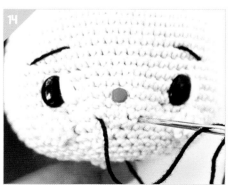

HAIR

Large Hair Piece

Round 1: With Color C and hook for Hair, make a magic ring, 6 sc in ring. (6sc)

Round 2: Inc in each st around. (12 sc)

Round 3: [Sc in next st, inc in next st] 6 times. (18 sc)

Round 4: [Sc in next 2 sts, inc in next st] 6 times. (24 sc)

Round 5: [Sc in next 3 sts, inc in next st] 6 times. (30 sc)

Round 6: *(Hair Strands)* [Sl st in next st, ch 20, starting in 2nd ch from hook, hdc in each ch across (19 hdc); working in Round 5, skip next st] 15 times, sl st in same st as first sl st. (15 Hair Strands) *(image 17)*

Fasten off, leaving a long tail for sewing.

Small Hair Piece

Round 1: With Color C and hook for Hair, make a magic ring, 6 sc in ring. (6 sc)

Round 2: Inc in each st around. (12 sc)

Round 3: [Sc in next st, inc in next st] 6 times. (18 sc)

Round 4: [Sc in next 2 sts, inc in next st] 6 times. (24 sc)

Round 5: (Hair Strands) [Sl st in next st, ch 15, starting in 2nd ch from hook, hdc in each ch across (14 hdc); working in Round 4, skip next st] 12 times, sl st in same st as first sl st. (12 Hair Strands) *(image 18)*

Fasten off, leaving a long tail for sewing.

Attaching Hair

1. Position Large Hair Piece on Head, with wrong side up, so that the Hair Strands fall naturally over the Head. Sew around the crown to secure. *(image 19)*

2. Place Small Hair Piece on top of Large Hair Piece, with right side up, and sew around the crown to secure. *(image 20 & 21)*

3. Adjust the Hair Strands with your fingers, either smoothing them out or making them curlier. *(image 22)*

LEGS & BODY

Note: *The Legs and Body are worked in one piece.*

First Leg

Round 1: With Color G, ch 8; starting in 2nd ch from hook, sc in next 6 ch, 3 sc in last ch; working on other side of starting chain, sc in next 6 ch. (15 sc)

Round 2: Inc in first st, sc in next 6 sts, inc in next 2 sts, sc in next 5 sts, inc in last st. (19 sc)

Round 3: Working in **back loops** only, sc in each st around. (19 sc)

Round 4: Working in both loops, sc in each st around. (19 sc)

Round 5: Sc in next 8 sts, [inv-dec] 3 times, sc in next 5 sts. (16 sc)

Round 6: Sc in next 7 sts, [inv-dec] 4 times, sc in the last st. (12 sc)

Change to Color D.

Rounds 7-11: (5 rounds) Sc in each st around. (12 sc)

Change to Color E.

Round 12: Inc in each st around. (24 sc)

Change to Color D.

Round 13: Sc in each st around. (24 sc)

Fasten off.

Stuff Leg firmly. *(image 23)*

Second Leg

Repeat instructions for First Leg but do not fasten off.

BODY

Joining Round: Working on Second Leg, ch 2; working on First Leg, with foot facing forward, sc in st at inside Leg, sc in next 23 sts; working in ch-2, sc in next 2 ch; working on Second Leg, sc in next 24 sts; working in unused loops on other side of ch-2, sc in next 2 ch; working on First Leg, sc in next 11 sts. *(image 24 & 25)*

Mark last st worked as new end of round.

Round 2: Sc in next 3 sts, [inv-dec] 12 times, sc in next 3 sts, [inv-dec] 5 times, sc in next 2 sts, [inv-dec] 5 times. (30 sc) Start stuffing legs. *(image 26)*

Rounds 3-7: *(5 rounds)* Sc in each st around. (30 sc)

Change to Color E.

Round 8: Sc in each st around. (30 sc)

Round 9: Working in **back loops** only, sc in each st around. (30 sc)

Change to Color D.

Rounds 10-12: *(3 rounds)* Sc in each st around. (30 sc)

Change to Color E.

Rounds 13-14: *(2 rounds)* Sc in each st around. (30 sc)

Change to Color D.

Rounds 15-16: *(2 rounds)* Sc in each st around. (30 sc)

Round 17: [Sc in next 3 sts, inv-dec] 6 times. (24 sc)

Fasten off, leaving a long tail for sewing. *(image 27)*
Stuff Body.

Pants Cuffs

Note: *Round 1 is worked around Round 8 on each Leg using Surface Single Crochet.*

Round 1: Holding Legs upside down, join Color D with standing sc to any st on Round 8, sc in next 12 sts; join with sl st to first sc. (13 sc)

Round 2: Ch 1, inc in first st, [sc in next st, inc in next st] 5 times, sc in last 2 sts. (19 sc)

Fasten off with Needle Join. *(image 28)*
Repeat on other Leg.

Shirt

Note: *Round 1 is worked in the unused front loops of Round 8 on Body.*

Round 1: Holding Body upside down, join Color E with standing sc to st at center back on Round 8, sc in next 8 sts, inc in next st, [sc in next 9 sts, inc in next st] around, join with sl st to first sc. (33 sc) *(image 29)*

Change to Color D.

Round 2: Ch 1, [sc in next 10 sts, inc in next st] around; join with sl st to first sc. (36 sc) *(image 30)*

Round 3: Ch 1, [sc in next 11 sts, inc in next st] around; join with sl st to first sc. (39 sc)

Round 4: Ch 1, [sc in next 12 sts, inc in next st] around; join with sl st to first sc. (42 sc)

Rounds 5-6: (2 rounds) Ch 1, sc in each st around; join with sl st to first sc. (42 sc)

Fasten off and weave in ends. *(image 31)*

Shoes & Body Details

1. With Color F and yarn needle, embroider backstitches around base of each Shoe. *(image 32)*

2. With Color F and yarn needle, embroider backstitches between the stripes on Round 12 of the Body. *(image 33)*

3. With Color D, make one long vertical straight stitch from top to bottom of Shirt, adding small stitches to hold the line in place. *(image 34, 35 & 36)*

4. Buttons - With Color H and yarn needle, make 3 French Knots, spaced evenly along vertical stitch on Body. For each French Knot, wrap yarn 5 times around needle. *(image 37, 38 & 39)*

COLLAR

Row 1: With Color D, ch 36, starting in 2nd ch from hook, dec *(using first 2 ch)*, sc in next 31 ch, dec *(using last 2 ch)*. (33 sc)

Rows 2: Ch 1, turn, dec *(using first 2 sts)*, sc in next 29 sts, dec *(using last 2 sts)*. (31 sc)

Fasten off, leaving a long tail for sewing. *(image 40)*

ARM (Make 2)

Round 1: With Color G, make a magic ring, 6 sc in ring. (6 sc)

Round 2: Inc in each st around. (12 sc)

Rounds 3-4: *(2 rounds)* Sc in each st around. (12 sc)

Round 5: [Inv-dec] 3 times, sc in next 6 sts. (9 sc)

Change to Color D.

Rounds 6-11: (6 rounds) Sc in each st around. (9 sc)

Change to Color E.

Round 12: Sc in each st around. (9 sc)

Change to Color D.

Round 13: Sc in each st around. (9 sc)

Fasten off, leaving a long tail for sewing.

Stuff arms lightly.

Sleeve Cuff

Note: *Round 1 is worked around Round 7 on each Arm using Surface Single Crochet.*

Round 1: Holding Arm upside down, join Color D with standing sc to any st on Round 7, sc in next 9 sts; join with sl st to first sc. (10 sc)

Round 2: Ch 1, inc in first st, sc in next st, [inc in next st, sc in next st] 4 times. (15 sc)

Fasten off with Needle Join and weave in ends.

Repeat on other Arm. *(image 41)*

HELMET

Hint: *Use 2 separate balls of yarn – holding one strand from each.*

Rounds 1-8: With double strand of Color E and hook for Helmet, repeat Rounds 1-8 of Head.

Rounds 9-14: *(6 rounds)* Sc in each st around. (48 sc)

Round 15: Working in **back loops** only, [sc in next st, inc in next st] around. (72 sc)

Round 16: Ch 1, hdc in each st around; join with sl st to first hdc. (72 hdc)

Visor Row: Ch 1, sc in next 16 sts. Leave remaining sts unworked. (16 sc)

Last Round: (Edging) Ch 1, turn, sc in each st across; working in Round 16, sl st in each st around. (16 sc & 56 sl sts)

Fasten off with Needle Join and weave in ends.

Vertical Ridges (using Surface Single Crochet)

Divide the Helmet into 5 equal "segments" – from crown to brim.

Hint: *A contrasting color yarn can be used as a guide to keep straight lines. Remove the yarn when the ridges are complete. (image 42)*

For each Ridge:

Using hook for Helmet, join double strand of Color E with standing sc to Round 1 at crown, work sc-sts in a straight line down to brim.

Fasten off and weave in ends.

Repeat until 5 ridges are made. *(image 43)*

Badge

Row 1: With Color I, ch 8, starting in 2nd ch from hook, sc in each ch across. (7 sc)

Rows 2-4: *(3 rows)* Ch 1, turn, sc in each st across. (7 sc)

Row 5: Ch 1, turn, skip first sc, sc in next 4 sts, dec (using last 2 sts). (5 sc)

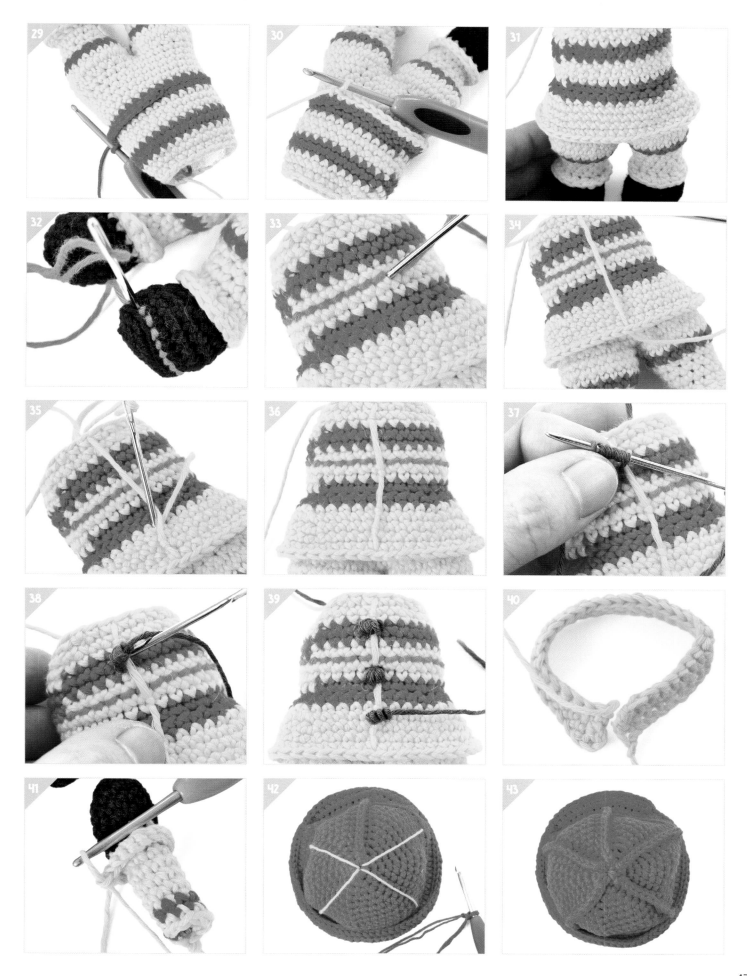

Row 6: Ch 1, turn, skip first sc, sc in next 2 sts, dec (using last 2 sts). (3 sc)

Edging Row: Working in sides of rows, sc in each of next 5 rows; working on other side of starting chain, sc in first ch, ch 3, sc in 2nd ch from hook, sc in next ch, sl st in same st on starting ch (point made), sc in next ch, skip next ch, (2 hdc, dc, ch 1, dc, 2 hdc) in next (center) ch, skip next ch, sc in next ch, sl st in last ch, ch 3, sc in 2nd ch from hook, sc in next ch, sc in same ch on starting ch (point made); working in sides of rows, sc in next 5 rows; join with sl st to first sc on Row 6. *(image 44)*

Fasten off, leaving a long tail for sewing.

Fire Logo

Large Flame: With Color F, ch 7, sl st in 2nd ch from hook, sc in next ch, hdc in next ch, dc in next 2 ch, (dc, sl st) in last ch.

Small Flame: *Ch 5, sl st in 2nd ch from hook, sc in next ch, hdc in next ch, dc in next ch, sl st in same last ch on Large Flame; repeat from * once more.

Fasten off, leaving a long tail for sewing.

Finishing the Helmet

1. Position the Fire Logo (with Large Flame hanging down) and sew only the Small Flames to the Badge. *(image 45)*

2. Fold the Large Flame up, and sew in place. *(image 46)*

3. With Color D and yarn needle, embroider a few straight stitches on each flame. *(image 47)*

4. Using long tail, sew Badge to center front of Helmet. *(image 48)*

FINAL DOLL ASSEMBLY

1. Sew the Body to the finished Head, adding more stuffing before finishing. *(image 49)*

2. Sew on Collar around neck. *(image 50)*

3. Position the Arms and sew in place, tucking them under the Collar. *(image 51)*

4. Place Helmet on Head. *(image 52)*

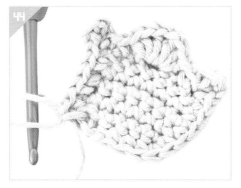
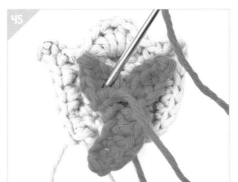

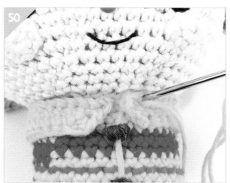

Austin
The Astronaut

Austin enjoys long showers, eating ice cream and cycling into the sunset. But ever since he was recruited on board the space shuttle, he has had to give up on his favorite things. He sure doesn't mind though. "To achieve your dreams, you sometimes have to make sacrifices," he says.

MATERIALS & TOOLS

HELLO Cotton Yarn

» **Main Color (MC):** Powder Peach (163) - for Head
» **Color A:** White (154) - for Eye Whites & Rocket
» **Color B:** Baby Pink (101) - for Cheeks
» **Color C:** Turquoise (134) - for Hair
» **Color D:** Light Gray (175) - for Helmet & Space Suit (Body, Legs & Arms)
» **Color E:** Off-White (155) - for Arms, Legs & Control Panel
» **Color F:** Blue (148) - for Helmet, Space Suit Detailing & Rocket Window
» **Color G:** Bright Orange (118) - for Space Suit Detailing
» **Color H:** Cherry Red (113) - for Rocket Tail Fins
» **Color I:** Dark Gray (176) - for Rocket & Window
» **Color J:** Mint Green (138) - for Control Panel

Hook Sizes

» 3mm hook – Main Hook
» 3.5mm hook – for Helmet

Other

» Stitch markers
» Yarn needle
» Stuffing
» Craft Glue
» Pins
» Safety Eyes - Black Oval 3/8" (10mm) x 2
» Scrapbooking Brad - Orange 5/32" (4mm) x 1 - for Nose
» DMC Embroidery Floss - Black
» Embroidery Needle

FINISHED SIZE
Astronaut - About 7⅔" (19.5cm) tall
Rocket - About 4¼" (11cm) tall

SKILL LEVEL
Intermediate

PATTERN NOTES

The smaller size hook is used throughout, unless otherwise stated.

SPECIAL STITCHES

Small Bobble (small bob) (refer to Special Crochet Stitches) : Yarn over, insert hook in stitch or space specified and pull up a loop (3 loops on hook), yarn over and draw through 2 loops on hook *(2 loops remain)*; *yarn over and insert hook in same stitch or space and pull up a loop, yarn over and draw through two loops on hook; repeat from * 2 times more *(5 loops on hook)*, yarn over and draw through all 5 loops; ch 1 to secure.

Note: The ch-1 does not count as a stitch and is skipped when working the next round.

AUSTIN

HEAD

Round 1: With MC, make a magic ring, 6 sc in ring. (6 sc)

Round 2: Inc in each st around. (12 sc)

Round 3: [Sc in next st, inc in next st] 6 times. (18 sc)

Round 4: [Sc in next 2 sts, inc in next st] 6 times. (24 sc)

Round 5: [Sc in next 3 sts, inc in next st] 6 times. (30 sc)

Round 6: [Sc in next 4 sts, inc in next st] 6 times. (36 sc)

Round 7: [Sc in next 5 sts, inc in next st] 6 times. (42 sc)

Round 8: [Sc in next 6 sts, inc in next st] 6 times. (48 sc)

Round 9: [Sc in next 7 sts, inc in next st] 6 times. (54 sc)

Round 10: [Sc in next 8 sts, inc in next st] 6 times. (60 sc)

Rounds 11-21: *(11 rounds)* Sc in each st around. (60 sc)

Round 22: [Sc in next 8 sts, inv-dec] 6 times. (54 sc) *(image 1)*

Round 23: [Sc in next 7 sts, inv-dec] 6 times. (48 sc)

Round 24: [Sc in next 6 sts, inv-dec] 6 times. (42 sc)

Add Facial Features:

1. Nose - position brad at front of Head (about 27th stitch on Round 20) and lock in place. *(image 2 & 3)*

2. Eyes - position on Round 19, about 6 stitches from either side of Nose and secure in place. *(image 4 & 5)*

3. Eye Whites - using Color A and yarn needle, make 3-4 vertical straight stitches (the same height as Eyes) to the left of each Eye. Knot and secure the yarn on the inside of the Head. *(image 6)*

Continue crocheting:

Round 25: [Sc in next 5 sts, inv-dec] 6 times. (36 sc)

Round 26: [Sc in next 4 sts, inv-dec] 6 times. (30 sc)

Round 27: [Sc in next 3 sts, inv-dec] 6 times. (24 sc)

Start stuffing Head, adding more as you go.

Round 28: [Sc in next 2 sts, inv-dec] 6 times. (18 sc)

Round 29: [Sc in next st, inv-dec] 6 times. (12 sc)

Round 30: [Inv dec] 6 times. (6 sc) Fasten off.

Close the opening securely and leave a long tail (for Eye Indentations). *(image 7)*

Cheek (Make 2)

Round 1: With Color B, make a magic ring, 6 sc in ring. (6 sc)

Fasten off with Needle Join, leaving a long tail for sewing.

FINISHING THE FACE

Eye Indentations

Using long tail on Head and yarn needle:

1. Bring needle up from base of Head and out next to the nose-side of Eye. *(image 8)*

2. Insert needle in next stitch, bringing it out at base of Head. Gently tug yarn to create a slight indentation at the Eye. *(image 9)*

3. Repeat steps 1 & 2 for other Eye. *(image 10 & 11)*

4. Secure yarn tail with a knot at base of Head and trim excess yarn.

Cheeks - Position the Cheeks below each Eye and sew in place, bringing the yarn out at base of Head. Secure with a knot and trim excess yarn. *(image 12)*

Eyebrows & Mouth

Using Black Embroidery Floss and needle:

1. Bring needle up from base of Head and embroider Eyebrows above each Eye – by making a diagonal straight stitch from Round 16 to Round 17, about 4 stitches long. *(image 13)*

2. After Eyebrows, bring needle down through Head to create a Mouth on Round 22, centered under the Nose – by making a loose horizontal straight stitch, about 3 stitches long, bringing needle out at base of Head. Tie ends in a knot to secure and trim excess yarn. *(image 14)*

3. Optional: Apply glue on Mouth, and use pins to shape the smile while the glue dries. *(image 15 & 16)*

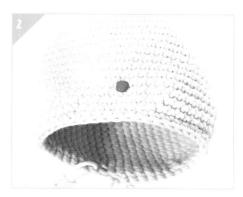

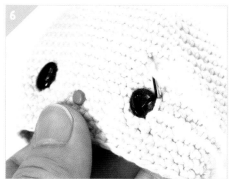
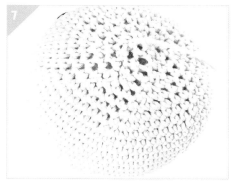
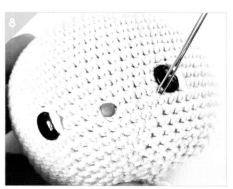

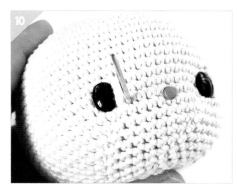

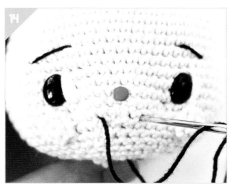

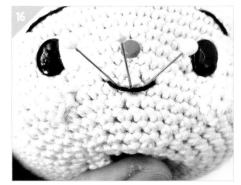

HAIR

Row 1: With Color C, ch 11, starting in 2nd ch from hook, dc in each st across. (10 dc)

Rows 2-7: *(6 rows)* Ch 1, turn, working in **back loops** only, [sc in next st, dc in next st] across. (5 sc & 5 dc)

Row 8: Ch 9, starting in 2nd ch from hook, [sc in next st, dc in next st] across. (4 sc & 4 dc)

Rows 9-12: *(4 rows)* Ch 1, turn, working in **back loops** only, [sc in next st, dc in next st] across. (4 sc & 4 dc) *(image 17)*

Fasten off, leaving a long tail for sewing.

Attaching Hair

Position Hair on Head (the bangs should be about 3 rounds above the Eyes) and using long tail and yarn needle, sew in place. *(image 18)*

HELMET

Rounds 1-10: With Color D and Helmet hook, repeat Rounds 1-10 of Head.

Rounds 11-23: *(13 rounds)* Sc in each st around. (60 sc)

Place Head into Helmet before continuing.

Round 24: [Sc in next 8 sts, inv-dec] 6 times. (54 sc)

Round 25: [Sc in next 7 sts, inv-dec] 6 times. (48 sc) *(image 19)*

Fasten off, leaving a long tail for sewing.

Ear Muff (Make 2)

Round 1: With Color F, make a magic ring, 6 sc in ring. (6 sc)

Round 2: Working in **back loops** only, inc in each st around. (12 sc)

Round 3: Working in **back loops** only, [sc in next st, inc in next st] 6 times. (18 sc)

Round 4: Working in **back loops** only, [sc in next 2 sts, inc in next st] 6 times. (24 sc)

Round 5: Working in **back loops** only, sc in each st around. (24 sc)

Fasten off, leaving a long tail for sewing. *(image 20)*

Head Panel

Round 1: With Color F, ch 10; starting in 2nd ch from hook, sc in next 8 ch, 3 sc in last ch; working on other side of starting chain, sc in next 8 ch. (19 sc)

Round 2: Inc in the first st, sc in the next 7 sts, inc in the next 2 sts, sc in next 8 sts, inc in last st. (23 sc) *(image 21)*

Fasten off, leaving a long tail for sewing.

Round 3: Working in back loops only, sc in each st around. (23 sc)

Finishing the Helmet

1. Using long tail of Helmet and yarn needle, sew Helmet to Head with small backstitches.

2. Position Ear Muffs on each side of Helmet and sew in place. *(image 22)*

3. Center Head Panel on top of Helmet and sew in place. *(image 23)*

LEGS & BODY

***Note**: The Legs and Body are worked in one piece.*

First Leg

Round 1: With Color E, ch 9; starting in 2nd ch from hook, sc in next 7 ch, 3 sc in last ch, working on other side of starting chain, sc in next 7 ch. (17 sc)

Round 2: Inc in the first st, sc in next 7 sts, inc in next 2 sts, sc in next 6 sts, inc in the last st. (21 sc)

Round 3: Inc in the first st, sc in next 9 sts, inc in next 2 sts, sc in next 8 sts, inc in the last st. (25 sc)

Round 4: Working in **back loops** only, sc in each st around. (25 sc)

Round 5: Sc in each st around. (25 sc)

Round 6: Sc in next 10 sts, inv-dec in next 3 sts, sc in next 9 sts. (22 sc)

Round 7: Sc in next 8 sts, inv-dec in next 4 sts, sc in next 6 sts. (18 sc) *(image 24)*

Rounds 8-11: *(4 rounds)* Sc in each st around. (18 sc)

Change to Color D.

Round 12: Working in **back loops** only, sc in each st around. (18 sc)

Rounds 13-14: *(2 rounds)* Sc in each st around. (18 sc)

Fasten off. Stuff Leg firmly. *(image 25)*

Second Leg

Repeat instructions for First Leg but do not fasten off.

Body

Joining Round: Working on Second Leg, ch 2; working on First Leg, with foot facing forward, sc in st at inside Leg, sc in next 17 sts; working in ch-2, sc in next 2 ch; working on Second Leg, sc in next 18 sts; working in unused loops on other side of ch-2, sc in next 2 ch; working on First Leg, sc in next 9 sts. *(image 26 & 27)*

Mark last st worked as new end of round.

Round 2: Sc in each st around. (40 sc)

Change to Color G.

Rounds 3-4: *(2 rounds)* Sc in each st around. (40 sc) *(image 28)*

Change to Color D.

Round 5: Inc in first st, sc in next 20 sts, inc in next st, sc in next 18 sts. (42 sc).

Round 6: Inc in first st, sc in next 21 sts, inc in next st, sc in next 19 sts. (44 sc).

Rounds 7-13: *(7 rounds)* Sc in each st around. (44 sc)

Round 14: Inv-dec *(using first 2 sts)*, sc in next 21 sts, inv-dec, sc in next 19 sts. (42 sc).

Round 15: [Sc in next 5 sts, inv-dec] around. (36 sc)

Round 16: [Sc in next 4 sts, inv-dec] around. (30 sc)

Fasten off, leaving a long tail for sewing.

Stuff Body. *(image 29)*

Boot Cuff

Round 1: Holding Legs upside down, working in unused front loops of Round 11, join Color E with standing sc to any stitch at back of Boot, sc in next 18 sts; join with sl st to first sc. (19 sc) *(image 30)*

Fasten off and weave in ends.

Repeat on other Leg.

Boot Detail

1. With Color G and yarn needle, sew a row of backstitches on Round 10 of each Leg.

2. Repeat with Color F, on Round 9 of each Leg. *(image 31)*

CONTROL PANEL

Row 1: With Color E, ch 12, starting in 2nd ch from hook, sc in each st across. (11 sc)

Rows 2-6: (5 rows) Ch 1, turn, sc in each st across. (11 sc)

Work continues in Rounds.

Round 7: Ch 1, turn, sc in each st across; working in sides of rows, sc in each of next 6 rows; working on other side of starting ch, sc in 11 ch; working in sides of rows, sc in each of next 6 rows (34 sc).

Round 8: Working in **back loops** only, sc in each st around (34 sc). *(image 32)*

Fasten off, leaving a long tail for sewing.

Control Panel Details

Green Circle

Round 1: With Color J, make a magic ring, 7 sc in ring. (7 sc)

Fasten off with Needle Join, leaving a long tail for sewing.

Green Square

Row 1: With Color J, ch 6, starting in 2nd ch from hook, sc in each st across. (5 sc)

Rows 2-3: (2 rows) Ch 1, turn, sc in each st across. (5 sc)

Fasten off, leaving a long tail for sewing.

Control Panel Assembly

1. Using Color G, make 2 French Knots (wrapping yarn 4 times around needle) on the Green Square.

2. Position and sew Green Circle and Green Square onto the Control Panel.

3. Using Color G, embroider a zig-zag line below the Green Circle.

4. With Color F, make three French Knots (wrapping yarn 3 times around needle) on Control Panel. Tie the ends together at the back to secure. *(image 33)*

5. Position and sew Control Panel to front of Body, adding stuffing before finishing. *(image 34)*

ARM (Make 2)

Round 1: With Color E, make a magic ring, 6 sc in ring. (6 sc)

Round 2: Inc in each st around. (12 sc)

Round 3: [Sc in next 3 sts, inc in next st] around. (15 sc)

Rounds 4-5: *(2 rounds)* Sc in each st around. (15 sc)

Round 6: Small bob in first st (thumb), sl st in next st, [inv-dec] 2 times, sc in next 9 sts. (11 sc, 1 small bobble & 1 sl st)

Round 7: Sc in next st, inv-dec, sc in next 10 sts. (12 sc)

Rounds 8-10: (3 rounds) Sc in each st around. (12 sc)

Change to Color D.

Round 11: Working in **back loops** only, sc in each st around. (12 sc) *(image 35)*

Rounds 12-15: *(4 rounds)* Sc in each st around. (12 sc)

Fasten off, leaving a long tail for sewing.

Stuff arms lightly.

Sleeve Cuff

Note: *Round 1 is worked in the unused front loops of Round 10 on Arm.*

Round 1: Holding Arm upside down, join Color E with standing sc to start of Round 10, sc in next 12 sts. (13 sc) *(image 36)*

Fasten off with Needle Join and weave in ends.

Repeat on other Arm.

Arm Stripes

1. With Color F and yarn needle, embroider backstitches on Round 7 of each Arm.

2. With Color G, embroider backstitches on Round 14.

Repeat Step 1 & 2 on other Arm. *(image 37)*

FINAL DOLL ASSEMBLY

1. Sew Body to finished Head, adding more stuffing before finishing. *(image 38)*

2. Position the Arms, with thumbs facing forward, and sew in place. *(image 39)*

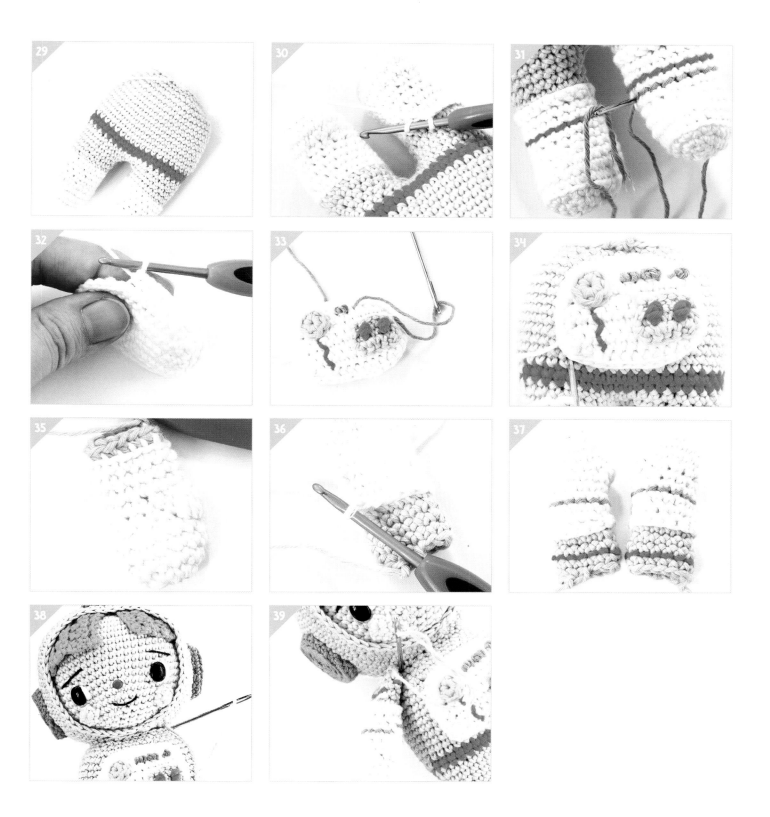

ROCKET

Round 1: With Color H, make a magic ring, 3 sc in ring. (3 sc)

Round 2: Inc in each st around. (6 sc)

Round 3: [Sc in next st, inc in next st] 3 times. (9 sc)

Round 4: Sc in each st around. (9 sc)

Round 5: [Sc in next 2 sts, inc in next st] 3 times. (12 sc)

Round 6: Sc in each st around. (12 sc)

Round 7: [Sc in next 3 sts, inc in next st] 3 times. (15 sc)

Change to Color A.

Round 8: [Sc in next 4 sts, inc in next st] 3 times. (18 sc)

Round 9: [Sc in next 5 sts, inc in next st] 3 times. (21 sc)

Round 10: [Sc in next 6 sts, inc in next st] 3 times. (24 sc)

Rounds 11-24: *(14 rounds)* Sc in each st around. (24 sc)

Round 25: [Sc in next 6 sts, inv-dec] 3 times. (21 sc)

Round 26: [Sc in next 5 sts, inv-dec] 3 times. (18 sc)

Change to Color I.

Start stuffing Rocket.

Round 27: [Sc in next 4 sts, inv-dec] 3 times. (15 sc)

Round 28: [Sc in next 3 sts, inv-dec] 3 times. (12 sc)

Round 29: [Sc in next 2 sts, inv-dec] 3 times. (9 sc)

Round 30: Inv-dec around. (6 sc)

Fasten off, leaving a long tail.

Finish stuffing and close the opening securely, weaving in ends.

FIN (Make 6)

Row 1: With Color H, ch 7, starting in 2nd ch from hook, sc in each st across. (6 sc)

Row 2: Ch 1, turn, inc in first st, sc in next 4 sts, sl st in last st. (6 sc)

Row 3: Ch 1, turn, skip first sl st, sc in next 5 sts, inc in last st. (7 sc)

Row 4: Ch 1, turn, inc in first st, sc in next 5 sts, sl st in last st (7 sc)

Row 5: Ch 1, turn, skip first sl st, sc in next 6 sts, inc in last st. (8 sc)

Fasten off, leaving long tail for sewing. *(image 40)*

Assembling Tail Fins

1. Matching the shapes, whipstitch 2 Fins together around three sides, leaving one of the diagonal ends open. *(image 41 & 42)*

Repeat step 1 until three complete Tail Fins are made.

WINDOW

Round 1: With Color F, make a magic ring, 6 sc in ring. (6 sc)

Round 2: Inc in each st around. (12 sc)

Change to Color I.

Round 3: [Sc in next st, inc in next st] 6 times. (18 sc)

Round 4: Working in front loops only, sc in each st around. (18 sc)

Fasten off with Needle Join, leaving a long tail for sewing.

ROCKET ASSEMBLY

1. Sew Window onto the Rocket, between Rounds 10 to 16. *(image 43)*

2. Position the Tail Fins, evenly spaced around the lower part of the Rocket, and sew in place. *(image 44)*

Megan
The Exchange Student

New friends. New culture. An entirely new language. Megan can't wait to experience it all – it is the first time she is travelling to another country and she is as excited as can be!

MATERIALS & TOOLS

HELLO Cotton Yarn

» **Main Color (MC):** Powder Peach (163) - for Head, Arms & Legs
» **Color A:** White (154) - for Eye Whites
» **Color B:** Light Pink (102) - for Cheeks
» **Color C:** Coral (111) - for Hair
» **Color D:** Lavender (140) - for Body & Skirt
» **Color E:** Orchid (141) - for Body
» **Color F:** Off-White (155) - for Arms & Skirt
» **Color G:** Fuchsia (106) - for Bow Tie
» **Color H:** Purple (143) - for Skirt Pattern
» **Color I:** Turquoise (134) - for Skirt Pattern, Hair Tie & Clip
» **Color J:** Black (160) - for Legs & Bag
» **Color K:** Light Brown (128) - for Shoes

Hook Sizes

» 3mm hook
» 3.5mm hook – for Hair

Other

» Stitch markers
» Yarn needle
» Stuffing
» Craft Glue
» Pins
» Safety Eyes - Black Oval 3/8" (10mm) x 2
» Scrapbooking Brad - Orange 5/32" (4mm) x 1 - for Nose
» DMC Embroidery Floss - Black
» Embroidery Needle
» Mini Buttons x 2 - For Bag
» Sewing thread & needle

FINISHED SIZE
About 7" (18cm) tall

SKILL LEVEL
Intermediate

PATTERN NOTES

The smaller size hook is used throughout, unless otherwise stated.

SPECIAL STITCHES

Surface Single Crochet (refer to Tips & Techniques): With right side of crochet piece facing, work between the stitches. Start with a slip knot on the hook and insert it in specified stitch and out in next stitch; pull up a loop *(2 loops on hook)*; yarn over hook and draw through both loops on hook. *(Standing surface single crochet made)*

For following stitches, insert hook in stitch where the hook came out of and out again in next stitch; pull up a loop *(2 loops on hook)*; yarn over and draw through both loops. *(Surface single crochet made)*

MEGAN

HEAD

Round 1: With MC, make a magic ring, 6 sc in ring. (6 sc)

Round 2: Inc in each st around. (12 sc)

Round 3: [Sc in next st, inc in next st] 6 times. (18 sc)

Round 4: [Sc in next 2 sts, inc in next st] 6 times. (24 sc)

Round 5: [Sc in next 3 sts, inc in next st] 6 times. (30 sc)

Round 6: [Sc in next 4 sts, inc in next st] 6 times. (36 sc)

Round 7: [Sc in next 5 sts, inc in next st] 6 times. (42 sc)

Round 8: [Sc in next 6 sts, inc in next st] 6 times. (48 sc)

Round 9: [Sc in next 7 sts, inc in next st] 6 times. (54 sc)

Round 10: [Sc in next 8 sts, inc in next st] 6 times. (60 sc)

Rounds 11-21: *(11 rounds)* Sc in each st around. (60 sc)

Round 22: [Sc in next 8 sts, inv-dec] 6 times. (54 sc) *(image 1)*

Round 23: [Sc in next 7 sts, inv-dec] 6 times. (48 sc)

Round 24: [Sc in next 6 sts, inv-dec] 6 times. (42 sc)

Add Facial Features:

1. Nose - position brad at front of Head (about 27th stitch on Round 20) and lock in place. *(image 2 & 3)*

2. Eyes - position on Round 19, about 6 stitches from either side of Nose and secure in place. *(image 4 & 5)*

3. Eye Whites - using Color A and yarn needle, make 3-4 vertical straight stitches (the same height as Eyes) to the left of each Eye. Knot and secure the yarn on the inside of the Head. *(image 6)*

Continue crocheting:

Round 25: [Sc in next 5 sts, inv-dec] 6 times. (36 sc)

Round 26: [Sc in next 4 sts, inv-dec] 6 times. (30 sc)

Round 27: [Sc in next 3 sts, inv-dec] 6 times. (24 sc)

Start stuffing Head, adding more as you go.

Round 28: [Sc in next 2 sts, inv-dec] 6 times. (18 sc)

Round 29: [Sc in next st, inv-dec] 6 times. (12 sc)

Round 30: [Inv dec] 6 times. (6 sc) Fasten off.

Close the opening securely and leave a long tail (for Eye Indentations). *(image 7)*

Cheek (Make 2)

Round 1: With Color B, make a magic ring, 6 sc in ring. (6 sc)

Fasten off with Needle Join, leaving a long tail for sewing.

FINISHING THE FACE

Eye Indentations

Using long tail on Head and yarn needle:

1. Bring needle up from base of Head and out next to the nose-side of Eye. *(image 8)*

2. Insert needle in next stitch, bringing it out at base of Head. Gently tug yarn to create a slight indentation at the Eye. *(image 9)*

3. Repeat steps 1 & 2 for other Eye. *(image 10 & 11)*

4. Secure yarn tail with a knot at base of Head and trim excess yarn.

Cheeks - Position the Cheeks below each Eye and sew in place, bringing the yarn out at base of Head. Secure with a knot and trim excess yarn. *(image 12)*

Eyebrows & Mouth

Using Black Embroidery Floss and needle:

1. Bring needle up from base of Head and embroider Eyebrows above each Eye – by making a diagonal straight stitch from Round 16 to Round 17, about 4 stitches long. *(image 13)*

2. After Eyebrows, bring needle down through Head to create a Mouth on Round 22, centered under the Nose – by making a loose horizontal straight stitch, about 3 stitches long, bringing needle out at base of Head. Tie ends in a knot to secure and trim excess yarn. *(image 14)*

3. Optional: Apply glue on Mouth, and use pins to shape the smile while the glue dries. *(image 15 & 16)*

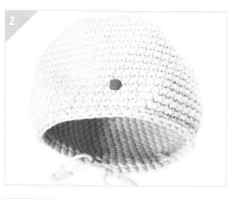

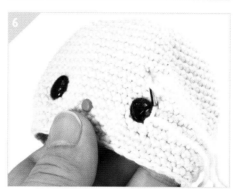

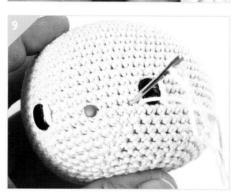

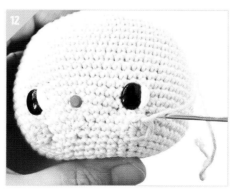

HAIR

Rounds 1-10: With Color C and larger hook, repeat Rounds 1-10 of the Head.

Rounds 11-13: *(3 rounds)* Sc in each st around. (60 sc)

Work continues in Rows.

Row 1: Ch 1, turn, sc in next 38 sts. (38 sc) Leave remaining sts unworked.

Rows 2-7: *(6 rows)* Ch 1, turn, sc in each st across. (38 sc) *(image 17)*

The final round is worked all around the Hair to neaten the edges.

Last Round: Ch 1, turn, *(wrong side facing)* sc in first st, sc in next 36 sts, 2 sc in last st; working in sides of rows, sc in each of next 5 rows; working across bangs, sc in next 23 sts; working in sides of rows, sc in each of next 5 rows, sc in same st as first st. (72 sc) *(image 18 & 19)*

Fasten off with Needle Join, leaving a long tail for sewing.

Pigtail (Make 2)

First Strand: With Color C and larger hook, ch 20, starting in 2nd ch from hook, hdc in 18 ch, (hdc, sl st) in last ch. (19 hdc & 1 sl st)

Second Strand: Ch 20, starting in 2nd ch from hook, hdc in 19 ch, sl st in same last ch on First Strand. (19 hdc)

Third Strand: Repeat Second Strand. (19 hdc) *(image 20)*

Fasten off, leaving a long tail for sewing.

Attaching & Finishing Hair

1. Position the Hair on the Head and sew in place using backstitches. *(image 21)*

2. Sew one Pigtail on each side of the Head, near Rounds 9-10 of the Hair. *(image 22)*

3. With Color I and yarn needle, sew 4 loops over each Pigtail for the Hair Tie. *(image 23)*

4. Sew an "X" on the left front of Hair on Rounds 10-13 (for Hairclip). *(image 24)*

BODY

Rounds 1-5: Using Color D, repeat Rounds 1-5 of Head.

Rounds 6-10: *(5 rounds)* Sc in each st around. (30 sc)

Change to Color E.

Rounds 11-18: *(8 rounds)* Sc in each st around. (30 sc)

Round 19: [Sc in next 3 sts, inv-dec] 6 times. (24 sc)

Fasten off, leaving a long tail for sewing.

Stuff body firmly. *(image 25)*

PLEATED SKIRT

Note: *When changing colors, do not cut the yarn.*

Row 1: With Color D, ch 10, starting in 2nd ch from hook, dc in next 4sts, hdc in next 3 sts, sc in next 2 sts. (9 sts)

Row 2: Ch 1, turn, working in **back loops** only, sc in next 2 sts, hdc in next 3 sts, dc in next 4 sts.

Row 3: Ch 1, turn, working in **back loops** only, dc in next 4sts, hdc in next 3 sts, sc in next 2 sts.

Rows 4-5: Change to Color F. Repeat Rows 2-3. *(image 26)*

Rows 6-7: Change to Color D. Repeat Rows 2-3.

Rows 8-9: Change to Color F. Repeat Rows 2-3.

Rows 10-33: (24 rows) Repeat Rows 6-9 six times more, ending with Color F. *(image 27)*

Edging Row: Change to Color D, working in sides of rows along top edge, sc in each row across. (33 sc) *(image 28)*

Fasten off, leaving a long tail for sewing.

Skirt Detail

Using Colors H & I and yarn needle, embroider horizontal and vertical lines in a plaid pattern, using small, evenly spaced backstitches. *(image 29, 30 & 31)*

Weave the ends in neatly at the back of the Skirt.

ARM (Make 2)

Round 1: With MC, make a magic ring, 6sc in ring. (6 sc)

Round 2: Inc in each st around. (12 sc)

Rounds 3-4: *(2 rounds)* Sc in each st around. (12 sc)

Round 5: [Inv-dec] 3 times, sc in next 6 sts. (9 sc)

Change to Color F.

Rounds 6-13: *(8 rounds)* Sc in each st around. (9 sc)

Fasten off, leaving a long tail for sewing.

Stuff arms lightly.

Sleeve Cuff

Note: *Round 1 is worked around Round 7 on each Arm using Surface Single Crochet.*

Round 1: Holding Arm upside down, join Color F with standing sc to any st on Round 7, sc in next 9 sts. (10 sc) *(image 32)*

Fasten off with Needle Join and weave in ends.

Repeat on other Arm.

LEG – WITH SHOE (Make 2)

Round 1: With Color K, ch 8; starting in 2nd ch from hook, sc in next 6 ch, 3 sc in last ch, working on other side of starting chain, sc in next 6 ch. (15 sc)

Round 2: Inc in first st, sc in next 6 sts, inc in next 2 sts, sc in next 5 sts, inc in last st. (19 sc)

Round 3: Working in **back loops** only, sc in each st around. (19 sc)

Round 4: Sc in each st around. (19 sc)

Round 5: Sc in next 8 sts, [inv-dec] 3 times, sc in next 5 sts. (16 sc)

Change to Color J.

Round 6: Working in **back loops** only, sc in next 7 sts, [inv-dec] 4 times, sc in the last st. (12 sc)

Rounds 7-11: *(5 rounds)* Sc in each st around. (12 sc)

Change to MC.

Rounds 12-13: *(2 rounds)* Sc in each st around. (12 sc)

Fasten off, leaving a long tail for sewing.

Stuff legs firmly.

Shoe Detail

Using Color J and yarn needle, embroider 5 long stitches - across 4 stitches - on the front of each Shoe. *(image 33)*

RIBBON

Bow

Row 1: With Color G, ch 4, starting in 2nd ch from hook, hdc in each ch across. (3 hdc)

Rows 2-12: *(11 rows)* Ch 1, turn, hdc in each st across (3 hdc)

Fasten off, leaving a long tail for sewing.

Tail

Row 1: With Color G, ch 13, starting in 2nd ch from hook, hdc in each ch across. (12 hdc)

Fasten off, leaving a long tail for sewing. *(image 34)*

Assembling Ribbon

1. Fold both ends of Bow towards the center, and whip stitch to secure shape.

2. With remaining yarn tail, make several loops tightly around middle of folded Bow (to create bow shape). *(image 35)*

3. Secure with a knot at back, and trim yarn ends.

4. Fold the Tail in a "V" shape. Set aside for assembly later. *(image 36)*.

BAG

Row 1: With Color J, ch 8, starting in 2nd ch from hook, hdc in each ch across. (7 hdc)

Rows 2-10: *(9 rows)* Ch 1, turn, hdc in each st across. (7 hdc)

Last Round: Ch 1, working in sides of rows, [sc in next row, 2 sc in next row] across; working on other side of starting ch, 2 sc in first ch, sc in each ch across to last ch, 2 sc in last ch; working in sides of rows, [2 sc in next row, sc in next row] across; working in Row 10, 2 sc in first st, sc in each st across to last st, 2 sc in last st; ch 30 *(for Strap)*. (48 sc & ch-30) *(image 37)*

Fasten off, leaving a long tail for sewing.

Finishing the Bag

1. Fold bottom edge (with Strap) up - to create a "pocket", and fold top edge over to create a flap. *(image 38)*

2. With tail from Strap and yarn needle, attach Strap to other side of Bag.

3. Use remaining tail to whipstitch the sides of the Bag closed. *(image 39)*

4. Sew mini buttons onto flap for decoration. *(image 40)*

FINAL DOLL ASSEMBLY

1. Sew Body to finished Head, adding more stuffing before finishing. *(image 41)*

2. Position the Arms and sew in place. *(image 42)*

3. Position the Legs and sew in place, adding more stuffing so Doll can stand when propped up against a wall. *(image 43)*

4. Wrap Skirt around Doll and using Color D long tail, sew to Body. *(image 44)*

5. Using Color F long tail, sew edges of Skirt together at back.

6. Sew the Ribbon Tail to center front at neck, then sew Ribbon Bow on top of it. *(image 45 & 46)*

7. Slip Bag over Doll. *(image 47)*

The Ballerina

Hours of practice will not dampen the spirit of this graceful ballerina.
Anna may only be eight, but she is already a rising star.

MATERIALS & TOOLS

HELLO Cotton Yarn

» **Main Color (MC):** Powder Peach (163) - for Head & Arms
» **Color A:** White (154) - for Eye Whites
» **Color B:** Light Pink (102) - for Cheeks
» **Color C:** Coral (111) - for Hair & Bun
» **Color D:** Dusty Blue (145) - for Dress & Shoes
» **Color E:** Off-White (155) - for Body & Legs

Hook Sizes

» 2mm hook – for Thread hook (for Diamond & Shoe Straps)
» 2.5mm hook– for Tiara
» 3mm hook – Main hook
» 3.5mm hook– for Hair

Other

» Stitch markers
» Yarn needle
» Stuffing
» Craft Glue
» Pins
» Safety Eyes - Black Oval 3/8" (10mm) x 2
» Scrapbooking Brad - Orange 5/32" (4mm) x 1 - for Nose
» DMC Embroidery Floss - Black
» Embroidery Needle
» White sewing thread & sewing needle
» Tulle Cloth 23½" (60cm) x 3" (8cm) - Mint (or color of your choice)
» Glitter crochet thread – Silver

FINISHED SIZE
About 8" (20cm) tall

SKILL LEVEL
Intermediate

PATTERN NOTES

The main hook is used throughout, unless otherwise stated.

SPECIAL STITCHES

Treble Crochet (tr) (refer to Special Crochet Stitches):

Yarn over hook twice, insert hook in stitch or space specified and pull up a loop (4 loops on hook), [yarn over and draw through 2 loops on hook] 3 times. Treble crochet stitch made.

ANNA

HEAD

Round 1: With MC, make a magic ring, 6 sc in ring. (6 sc)

Round 2: Inc in each st around. (12 sc)

Round 3: [Sc in next st, inc in next st] 6 times. (18 sc)

Round 4: [Sc in next 2 sts, inc in next st] 6 times. (24 sc)

Round 5: [Sc in next 3 sts, inc in next st] 6 times. (30 sc)

Round 6: [Sc in next 4 sts, inc in next st] 6 times. (36 sc)

Round 7: [Sc in next 5 sts, inc in next st] 6 times. (42 sc)

Round 8: [Sc in next 6 sts, inc in next st] 6 times. (48 sc)

Round 9: [Sc in next 7 sts, inc in next st] 6 times. (54 sc)

Round 10: [Sc in next 8 sts, inc in next st] 6 times. (60 sc)

Rounds 11-21: *(11 rounds)* Sc in each st around. (60 sc)

Round 22: [Sc in next 8 sts, inv-dec] 6 times. (54 sc) *(image 1)*

Round 23: [Sc in next 7 sts, inv-dec] 6 times. (48 sc)

Round 24: [Sc in next 6 sts, inv-dec] 6 times. (42 sc)

Add Facial Features:

1. Nose - position brad at front of Head (about 27ᵗʰ stitch on Round 20) and lock in place. *(image 2 & 3)*

2. Eyes - position on Round 19, about 6 stitches from either side of Nose and secure in place. *(image 4 & 5)*

3. Eye Whites - using Color A and yarn needle, make 3-4 vertical straight stitches (the same height as Eyes) to the left of each Eye. Knot and secure the yarn on the inside of the Head. *(image 6)*

Continue crocheting:

Round 25: [Sc in next 5 sts, inv-dec] 6 times. (36 sc)

Round 26: [Sc in next 4 sts, inv-dec] 6 times. (30 sc)

Round 27: [Sc in next 3 sts, inv-dec] 6 times. (24 sc)

Start stuffing Head, adding more as you go.

Round 28: [Sc in next 2 sts, inv-dec] 6 times. (18 sc)

Round 29: [Sc in next st, inv-dec] 6 times. (12 sc)

Round 30: [Inv dec] 6 times. (6 sc) Fasten off.

Close the opening securely and leave a long tail (for Eye Indentations). *(image 7)*

Cheek (Make 2)

Round 1: With Color B, make a magic ring, 6 sc in ring. (6 sc)

Fasten off with Needle Join, leaving a long tail for sewing.

FINISHING THE FACE

Eye Indentations

Using long tail on Head and yarn needle:

1. Bring needle up from base of Head and out next to the nose-side of Eye. *(image 8)*

2. Insert needle in next stitch, bringing it out at base of Head. Gently tug yarn to create a slight indentation at the Eye. *(image 9)*

3. Repeat steps 1 & 2 for other Eye. *(image 10 & 11)*

4. Secure yarn tail with a knot at base of Head and trim excess yarn.

Cheeks - Position the Cheeks below each Eye and sew in place, bringing the yarn out at base of Head. Secure with a knot and trim excess yarn. *(image 12)*

Eyebrows & Mouth

Using Black Embroidery Floss and needle:

1. Bring needle up from base of Head and embroider Eyebrows above each Eye – by making a diagonal straight stitch from Round 16 to Round 17, about 4 stitches long. *(image 13)*

2. After Eyebrows, bring needle down through Head to create a Mouth on Round 22, centered under the Nose – by making a loose horizontal straight stitch, about 3 stitches long, bringing needle out at base of Head. Tie ends in a knot to secure and trim excess yarn. *(image 14)*

3. Optional: Apply glue on Mouth, and use pins to shape the smile while the glue dries. *(image 15 & 16)*

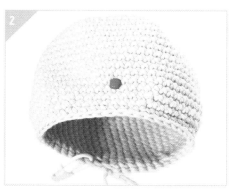

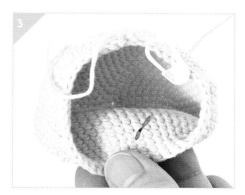

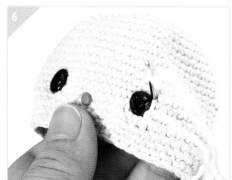

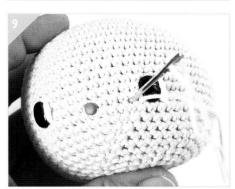

HAIR

Rounds 1-10: With Color C and Hair hook, repeat Rounds 1-10 of the Head.

Rounds 11-13: *(3 rounds)* Sc in each st around. (60 sc)

Work continues in Rows.

Row 1: Ch 1, turn, sc in next 38 sts. (38 sc) Leave remaining sts unworked.

Rows 2-7: *(6 rows)* Ch 1, turn, sc in each st across. (38 sc) *(image 17)*

Last Round: (Edging & Bangs) Working in sides of rows, sc in each of next 7 rows; working in Round 13, [5 dc in next st, skip next st] 11 times; working in sides of rows, sc in each of next 7 rows. *(image 18 & 19)*

Fasten off with Needle Join, leaving a long tail for sewing.

Hair Bun

Round 1: With Color C and Hair hook, make a magic ring, 6 sc in ring. (6 sc)

Round 2: Inc in each st around. (12 sc)

Round 3: [Sc in next st, inc in next st] 6 times. (18 sc)

Round 4: [Sc in next 2 sts, inc in next st] 6 times. (24 sc)

Rounds 5-8: *(4 rounds)* Sc in each st around. (24 sc)

Round 9: [Sc in next 2 sts, inv-dec] 6 times. (18 sc)

Fasten off, leaving a long tail for sewing.

Stuff Hair Bun firmly.

Tiara

Row 1: With Crochet Thread and Tiara hook, ch 17; starting in 2nd ch from hook, sc in each st across. (16 sc)

Row 2: Ch 1, turn, sc in each st across. (16 sc)

Last Row: Turn, *ch 6, sl st in 2nd ch from hook, sc in next ch, hdc in next ch, dc in next ch, tr in last ch; working on Row 2, skip next 3 sts, sl st in next st; repeat from * 3 times more. (4 points) *(image 20 & 21)*

Fasten off, leaving a long tail for sewing.

Attaching Hair

1. Position Hair on Head and using long tail and yarn needle, sew in place. *(image 22)*

2. Position the Hair Bun on top of Head, and sew in place. *(image 23)*

3. Wrap Tiara around Hair Bun and sew in place. *(image 24)*

BODY

Rounds 1-5: Using Color E, repeat Rounds 1-5 of Head.

Rounds 6-10: *(5 rounds)* Sc in each st around. (30 sc)

Change to Color D.

Round 11: Sc in each st around. (30 sc)

Round 12: Working in **back loops** only, sc in each st around. (30 sc)

Rounds 13-18: *(6 rounds)* Sc in each st around. (30 sc)

Round 19: [Sc in next 3 sts, inv-dec] 6 times. (24 sc)

Fasten off, leaving a long tail for sewing.

Stuff body firmly.

Skirt

Note: *Round 1 is worked in the unused front loops of Round 11 on Body.*

Round 1: Holding Body upside down, join Color D with standing sc to any st at center back, sc in same st, [inc in next st] 29 times, join with sl st to first sc. (60 sc) *(image 25 & 26)*

Rounds 2-4: *(3 rounds)* Ch 1, sc in each st around; join with sl st to first sc. (60 sc)

Round 5: Ch 1, [sc in next st, inc in next st] around; join with sl st to first sc. (90 sc) *(image 27)*

Fasten off and weave in ends. *(image 28)*

Diamond Applique

Row 1: With Crochet Thread and Thread hook, ch 6; starting in 2nd ch from hook, sc in next 5 ch. (5 sc)

Rows 2-5: (4 rows) Ch 1, turn, sc in each st across. (5 sc)

Fasten off, leaving a long tail for sewing.

ARM (Make 2)

Round 1: With MC, make a magic ring, 6 sc in ring. (6 sc)

Round 2: Inc in each st around. (12 sc)

Rounds 3-4: *(2 rounds)* Sc in each st around. (12 sc)

Round 5: [Inv-dec] 3 times, sc in next 6 sts. (9 sc)

Rounds 6-13: *(8 rounds)* Sc in each st around. (9 sc)

Fasten off, leaving a long tail for sewing.

Stuff Arm lightly.

Sleeve (Make 2)

Row 1: With Color D, ch 12; 2 hdc in 2nd ch from hook, [2 hdc in next ch] across. (22 hdc)

Fasten off, leaving a long tail for sewing. *(image 29)*

LEG - WITH SHOE (Make 2)

Round 1: With Color D, ch 8; starting in 2nd ch from hook, sc in next 6 ch, 3 sc in last ch; working on other side of starting chain, sc in next 6 ch. (15 sc)

Round 2: Inc in first st, sc in next 6 sts, inc in each of next 2 sts, sc in next 5 sts, inc in last st. (19 sc)

Round 3: Working in **back loops** only, sc in each st around. (19 sc)

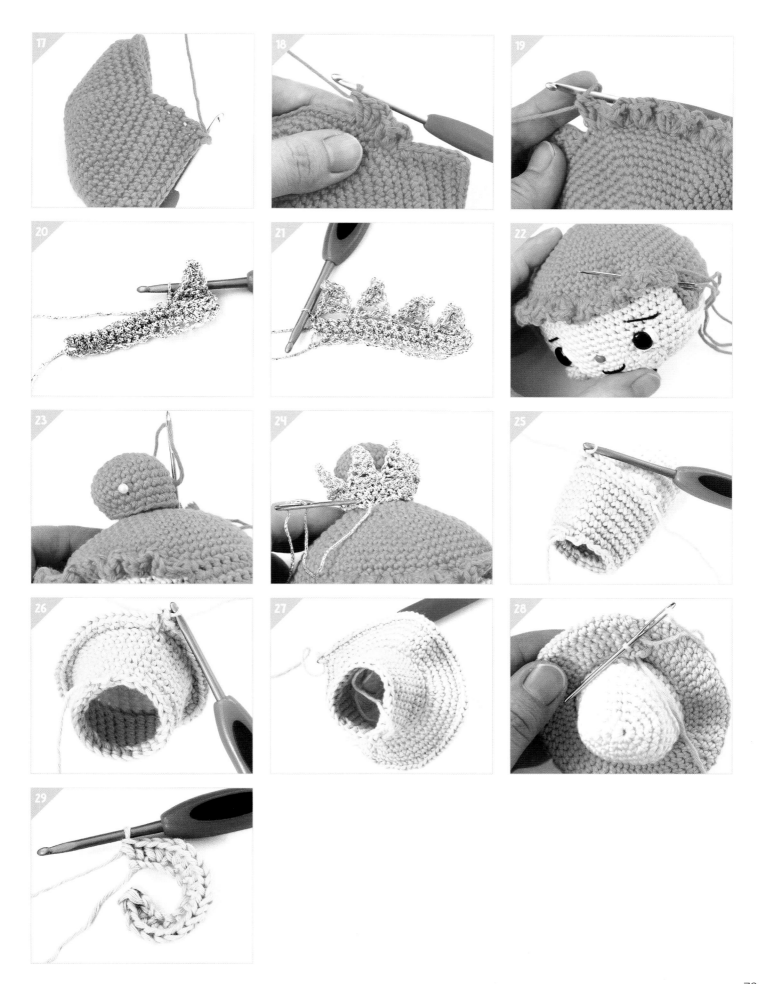

Round 4: Sc in each st around. (19 sc)

Round 5: Sc in next 8 sts, [inv-dec] 3 times, sc in next 5 sts. (16 sc)

Change to Color E.

Round 6: Working in **back loops** only, sc in next 7 sts, [inv-dec] 4 times, sc in last st. (12 sc)

Rounds 7-14: *(8 rounds)* Sc in each st around. (12 sc)

Fasten off, leaving a long tail for sewing.

Stuff legs firmly. *(image 30)*

Shoe Straps (Make 2)

With Crochet Thread and Thread hook, ch 27. Fasten off, leaving a long tail for sewing.

FINAL DOLL ASSEMBLY

1. Sew Body to finished Head, adding more stuffing before finishing. *(image 31)*

2. Attach the Tulle Tutu:

a. Fold Tulle in half length-wise. *(image 32)*

b. Wrap the Tulle around the Body under the Skirt, pinning the ends together at center back. *(image 33)*

c. Using pins to hold in place, make small tucks in the Tulle all around Body. *(image 34)*

d. Using sewing thread and needle, sew the Tulle Tutu in place. *(image 35)*

3. Position Arms and sew in place. *(image 36)*

4. Sew on Sleeves. *(image 37)*

5. Sew Diamond Applique on front of Body. *(image 38)*

6. Position Legs and sew in place, adding more stuffing so doll can stand when propped up against a wall. *(image 39)*

7. Wrap Shoe Straps around the Leg in an "X" and sew in place. *(image 40, 41 & 42)*

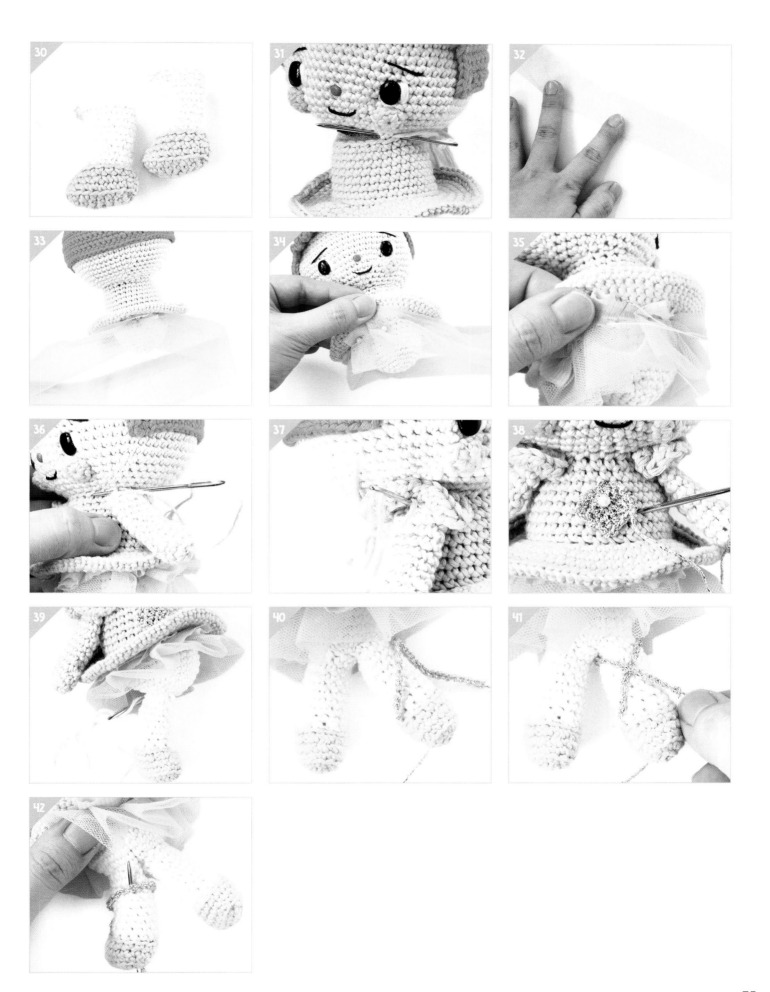

Grandpa & Grandma

Grandpa and Grandma are the sweetest couple ever. They have never been apart for longer than a day and will soon be celebrating their 50th year golden anniversary.

MATERIALS & TOOLS

HELLO Cotton Yarn

Grandpa

» **Main Color (MC):** Powder Peach (163) - for Head & Arms
» **Color A:** White (154) - for Eye Whites
» **Color B1:** Baby Pink (101) - for Cheeks
» **Color C:** Gray (159) - for Hair & Eyebrows
» **Color D:** Blue (148) - for Pants
» **Color E:** Sea Green (136) - for Vest
» **Color F:** Mustard (124) - for Patterns on Vest
» **Color G:** Beige (157) - for Shirt & Hat
» **Color H:** Tobacco (166) - for Shoes
» **Color I:** Brown (126) - for Soles of Shoes & Shoelaces

Grandma

» **Main Color (MC):** Powder Peach (163) - for Head, Arms & Legs
» **Color A:** White (154) - for Eye Whites
» **Color B2:** Light Pink (102) - for Cheeks
» **Color C:** Gray (159) - for Hair & Eyebrows
» **Color E:** Sea Green (136) - for Details on Shoes
» **Color G:** Beige (157) - for Cardigan
» **Color J:** Lilac (139) - for Dress & Shoes
» **Color K:** Off-White (155) - Underwear and Dress Hem

Hook Sizes

» 2mm hook – for Grandma's Appliqué
» 3mm hook – Main hook
» 3.5mm hook – for Hair

Other

» Stitch markers
» Yarn needle
» Stuffing
» Craft Glue
» Pins

For Each Doll

» Safety Eyes - Black Oval 3/8" (10mm) x 2
» Scrapbooking Brad - Orange 5/32" (4mm) x 1 - for Nose
» DMC Embroidery Floss – Black
» Embroidery Needle
» Jewelry wire – about 10" long
» Wire Cutter

For Grandma

» DMC Embroidery Floss - Yellow
» DMC Embroidery Floss - Ecru
» DMC Embroidery Floss - Sea Green
» White Mini Beads x 4 - for Earrings & Cardigan

FINISHED SIZE
Each Doll is about 7¼" (18.5cm) tall

SKILL LEVEL
Intermediate

PATTERN NOTES

The main size hook is used throughout, unless otherwise stated.

When working double crochet rows or rounds, the first ch-2 does not count as the first stitch. The first dc of a row is worked in the last stitch made on the previous row. The first dc of a round is worked in the same stitch as the previous round's join.

SPECIAL STITCHES

Surface Single Crochet (refer to Tips & Techniques): With right side of crochet piece facing, work between the stitches. Start with a slip knot on the hook and insert it in specified stitch and out in next stitch; pull up a loop (2 loops on hook); yarn over hook and draw through both loops on hook. (standing surface single crochet made)

For following stitches, insert hook in stitch where the hook came out of and out again in next stitch; pull up a loop (2 loops on hook); yarn over and draw through both loops. (Surface single crochet made)

Double Crochet Decrease (dc2tog) (refer to Special Crochet Stitches): Yarn over, insert hook in specified stitch or space and pull up a loop. Yarn over and draw through 2 loops on the hook. (2 loops remain) Yarn over, insert hook in next stitch or space and pull up a loop. Yarn over and draw through 2 loops on the hook. (3 loops remain) Yarn over and draw through all 3 loops on hook. (Double crochet decrease made)

Cluster (using 2 double crochet stitches) (2dc cl): Yarn over, insert hook in stitch or space specified and pull up a loop (3 loops on hook), yarn over and draw through 2 loops on hook (2 loops remain); yarn over and insert hook in same stitch or space and pull up a loop, yarn over and draw through two loops on hook (3 loops on hook), yarn over and draw through all 3 loops.

Cluster (using 3 double crochet stitches) (3dc cl): Yarn over, insert hook in stitch or space specified and pull up a loop (3 loops on hook), yarn over and draw through 2 loops on hook (2 loops remain); *yarn over and insert hook in same stitch or space and pull up a loop, yarn over and draw through two loops on hook; repeat from * once more (4 loops on hook), yarn over and draw through all 4 loops.

GRANDPA & GRANDMA

HEAD

Round 1: With MC, make a magic ring, 6 sc in ring. (6 sc)

Round 2: Inc in each st around. (12 sc)

Round 3: [Sc in next st, inc in next st] 6 times. (18 sc)

Round 4: [Sc in next 2 sts, inc in next st] 6 times. (24 sc)

Round 5: [Sc in next 3 sts, inc in next st] 6 times. (30 sc)

Round 6: [Sc in next 4 sts, inc in next st] 6 times. (36 sc)

Round 7: [Sc in next 5 sts, inc in next st] 6 times. (42 sc)

Round 8: [Sc in next 6 sts, inc in next st] 6 times. (48 sc)

Round 9: [Sc in next 7 sts, inc in next st] 6 times. (54 sc)

Round 10: [Sc in next 8 sts, inc in next st] 6 times. (60 sc)

Rounds 11-21: *(11 rounds)* Sc in each st around. (60 sc)

Round 22: [Sc in next 8 sts, inv-dec] 6 times. (54 sc) *(image 1)*

Round 23: [Sc in next 7 sts, inv-dec] 6 times. (48 sc)

Round 24: [Sc in next 6 sts, inv-dec] 6 times. (42 sc)

Add Facial Features:

1. Nose - position brad at front of Head (about 27th stitch on Round 20) and lock in place. *(image 2 & 3)*

2. Eyes - position on Round 19, about 6 stitches from either side of Nose and secure in place. *(image 4 & 5)*

3. Eye Whites - using Color A and yarn needle, make 3-4 vertical straight stitches (the same height as Eyes) to the left of each Eye. Knot and secure the yarn on the inside of the Head. *(image 6)*

Continue crocheting:

Round 25: [Sc in next 5 sts, inv-dec] 6 times. (36 sc)

Round 26: [Sc in next 4 sts, inv-dec] 6 times. (30 sc)

Round 27: [Sc in next 3 sts, inv-dec] 6 times. (24 sc)

Start stuffing Head, adding more as you go.

Round 28: [Sc in next 2 sts, inv-dec] 6 times. (18 sc)

Round 29: [Sc in next st, inv-dec] 6 times. (12 sc)

Round 30: [Inv dec] 6 times. (6 sc) Fasten off.

Close the opening securely and leave a long tail (for Eye Indentations). *(image 7)*

Cheek (Make 2)

Round 1: With Color B1 (for Grandpa) or Color B2 (for Grandma), make a magic ring, 6 sc in ring. (6 sc)

Fasten off with Needle Join, leaving a long tail for sewing.

Eyelid (Make 2)

Row 1: With MC, ch 5, starting in 2nd ch from hook, sc in each st across. (4 sc)

Fasten off, leaving a long tail for sewing.

Ear (Make 2)

Round 1: With MC, make a magic ring, 6 sc in ring. (6 sc)

Fasten off, leaving a long tail for sewing.

FINISHING THE FACE

Eye Indentations

Using long tail on Head and yarn needle:

1. Bring needle up from base of Head and out next to the nose-side of Eye. *(image 8)*

2. Insert needle in next stitch, bringing it out at base of Head. Gently tug yarn to create a slight indentation at the Eye. *(image 9)*

3. Repeat steps 1 & 2 for other Eye. *(image 10 & 11)*

4. Secure yarn tail with a knot at base of Head and trim excess yarn.

Cheeks - Position the Cheeks below each Eye and sew in place, bringing the yarn out at base of Head. Secure with a knot and trim excess yarn.

Mouth, Eyelids & Eyebrows

1. Using Black Embroidery Floss and needle, bring needle up from base of Head and embroider a Mouth on Round 22, centered under the Nose – by making a loose horizontal straight stitch, about 3 stitches long, bringing needle out at base of Head.

Tie ends in a knot to secure and trim excess yarn.

2. Optional: Apply glue on Mouth, and use pins to shape the smile while the glue dries.

3. Position the Eyelids above each Eye (slightly overlapping the top of the Eye), and sew in place.

4. Using Color C and yarn needle, bring needle up from base of Head and embroider Eyebrows above each Eye – by making a diagonal straight stitch from Round 16 to Round 17, about 4 stitches long. Bring needle out at base of Head, and tie ends in a knot to secure. Trim excess yarn. *(image 12)*

Ears - Sew an Ear to each side of the Head, about 6 stitches away from the Eye. *(image 13)*

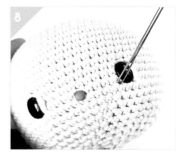
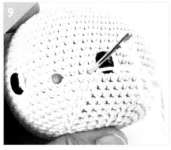

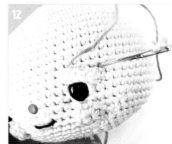

GRANDPA

HAIR

Row 1: With Color C and Hair hook, ch 38, starting in 2nd ch from hook, sc in each st across. (37 sc)

Rows 2-4: *(3 rows)* Ch 1, turn, working in **back loops** only, sc in each st across. (37 sc) *(image 14)*

Fasten off, leaving a long tail for sewing.

ARM (Make 2)

Round 1: With MC, make a magic ring, 6 sc in ring. (6 sc)

Round 2: Inc in each st around. (12 sc)

Rounds 3-4: *(2 rounds)* Sc in each st around. (12 sc)

Round 5: [Inv-dec] 3 times, sc in the next 6 sts. (9 sc)

Change to Color G.

Round 6: [Sc in next 2 sts, inc in next st] 3 times. (12 sc)

Round 7: [Sc in next 3 sts, inc in next st] 3 times. (15 sc)

Rounds 8-12: *(5 rounds)* Sc in each st around. (15 sc)

Round 13: [Sc in next 3 sts, inv-dec] 3 times. (12 sc)

Fasten off, leaving a long tail for sewing.

Stuff Arms lightly. *(image 15)*

LEGS & BODY

Note: The Legs and Body are worked in one piece.

First Leg

Round 1: With Color I, ch 6; starting in 2nd ch from hook, sc in next 4 ch, 3 sc in last ch, working on other side of starting chain, sc in next 4 ch. (11 sc)

Round 2: Inc in first st, sc in next 4 sts, inc in each of next 2 sts, sc in next 3 sts, inc in last st. (15 sc)

Change to Color H.

Round 3: Working in **back loops** only, sc in each st around. (15 sc)

Round 4: Sc in next 4 sts, [inv-dec] 4 times, sc in next 3 sts. (11 sc)

Round 5: Sc in next 3 sts, [inv-dec] 2 times, sc in next 4 sts. (9 sc)

Change to Color D.

Round 6: [Sc in next 2 sts, inc in next st] 3 times. (12 sc)

Round 7: [Sc in next 3 sts, inc in next st] 3 times. (15 sc)

Rounds 8-10: *(3 rounds)* Sc in each st around. (15 sc)

Fasten off. *(image 16)*

Stuff leg firmly.

Second Leg

Repeat instructions for First Leg but do not fasten off.

Body

Round1: *(Joining Legs)* Working on Second Leg, ch 3; working on First Leg, with foot facing forward, sc in st at inside Leg, sc in next 14 sts; working in ch-3, sc in next 3 ch, working on Second Leg, sc in next 15 sts; working in unused loops on other side of ch-3, sc in next 3 ch; working on First Leg, sc in next 7 sts. *(image 17 & 18)*

Mark last st worked as new end of round.

Rounds 2-7: *(6 rounds)* Sc in each st around. (36 sc)

Change to Color G.

Rounds 8-16: *(9 rounds)* Sc in each st around. (36 sc)

Round 17: [Sc in next 4 sts, inv-dec] 6 times. (30 sc)

Round 18: [Sc in next 3 sts, inv-dec] 6 times.

Fasten off, leaving a long tail for sewing. *(image 19)*

Stuff Body firmly.

VEST

Row 1: With Color E (leaving long tail for sewing), ch 31, starting in 2nd ch from hook, hdc in each ch across. (30 hdc)

Row 2: Ch 1, turn, working in **back loops** only, [2 hdc in next st, hdc in next 4 sts] 5 times, hdc in next 4 sts, 2 hdc in last st. (36 hdc)

Row 3: Ch 1, turn, working in **back loops** only, [2 hdc in next st, hdc in next 5 sts] 5 times, hdc in next 5 sts, 2 hdc in last st. (42 hdc)

Row 4: Ch 1, turn, working in **back loops** only, [2 hdc in next st, hdc in next 6 sts] 5 times, hdc in next 6 sts, 2 hdc in last st; join with sl st to first hdc. (48 hdc) *(image 20 & 21)*

Work continues in Rounds.

Round 5: Ch 1,working in **back loops** only, sc in each st around; join with sl st to first sc. (48 sc)

Change to Color F.

Round 6: Ch 1, working in **back loops** only, sc in each st around; join with sl st to first sc. (48 sc)

Change to Color E.

Round 7: Ch 1, sc in each st around; join with sl st to first sc. (48 sc)

Change to Color F.

Round 8: Ch 1, sc in each st around; join with sl st to first sc. (48 sc)

Change to Color E. (Fasten off Color F and tie ends together on the inside.)

Round 9: Ch 1, working in **back loops** only, hdc in each st around; join with sl st to first hdc. (48 hdc) *(image 22)*

Rounds 10-11: *(2 rounds)* Ch 1, hdc in each st around; join with sl st to first hdc. (48 hdc)

Round 12: Ch 1, sl st in each st around. (48 sl st)

Fasten off with Needle Join and weave in finishing end (not beginning long tail).

Vest Edging

Holding Vest upside Down, working in ends of rows of Rows 1-4, with Color F make a standing sc at base of Row 1, sc in same row, 2 sc in each of next 2 rows, sc in next Row, sc in join; working up other side, sc in next row, 2 sc in each of next 3 rows. (15 sc) *(image 23)*

Fasten off and weave in ends.

81

HAT

Round 1: With Color G, make a magic ring, ch 2, 10 dc in ring; join with sl st to first dc. (10 dc)

Round 2: Ch 2, 2 dc in each st around; join with sl st to first dc. (20 dc)

Round 3: Ch 2, dc in first st, 2 dc in next st, [dc in next st, 2 dc in next st] 9 times; join with sl st to first dc. (30 dc)

Round 4: Ch 2, dc in first st, dc in next st, 2 dc in next st, [dc in next 2 sts, 2 dc in next st] 9 times; join with sl st to first dc. (40 dc)

Round 5: Ch 2, dc in first st, dc in next 2 sts, 2 dc in next st, [dc in next 3 sts, 2 dc in next st] 9 times; join with sl st to first dc. (50 dc)

Round 6: Ch 2, dc in first st, dc in next 19 sts, 2 dc in each of next 10 sts, dc in next 20 sts; join with sl st to first dc. (60 dc)

Round 7: Ch 2, dc in each st around; join with sl st to first dc. (60 dc) *(image 24)*

Round 8: Ch 2, dc in first st, dc in next 19 sts, [dc2tog] 10 times, dc in next 20 sts; join with sl st to first dc. (50 dc) *(image 25)*

Fasten off, leaving a long tail for sewing.

FINAL DOLL ASSEMBLY

1. Position Hair strip across back of Head, above the Ears, between Rounds 12-16, and sew in place. *(image 26)*

2. Position Hat on top of Head, with puffed out part facing the front, and sew in place. *(image 27)*

3. Sew Body to finished Head, adding more stuffing before finishing. *(image 28)*

4. Slip Vest over Body, and secure in position with a few backstitches around the neck. *(image 29)*

5. Position the Arms and sew in place. *(image 30)*

6. With Color I and yarn needle, embroider an "X" on the top of each shoe (for shoelaces). *(image 31)*

7. Make Eye Glasses:

a. Cut 2 short pieces of jewelry wire measuring about 2" (5.5cm) each.

b. Wrap each wire piece around a pen (or any cylindrical object) to form neat rings. *(image 32)*

c. Cut a longer piece of wire measuring about 5½" (13.5cm). *(image 33)*

d. Leaving a short end, wrap the long wire piece around the one ring. Bend the short end to 90 degrees and insert this into the Head near the right Eye. *(image 34 &35)*

e. Gauge the distance between the Eyes, and wrap the other end of the long wire piece around the other ring. Trim the wire end and bend to 90 degrees and insert into Head near other Eye. *(image 36 & 37)*

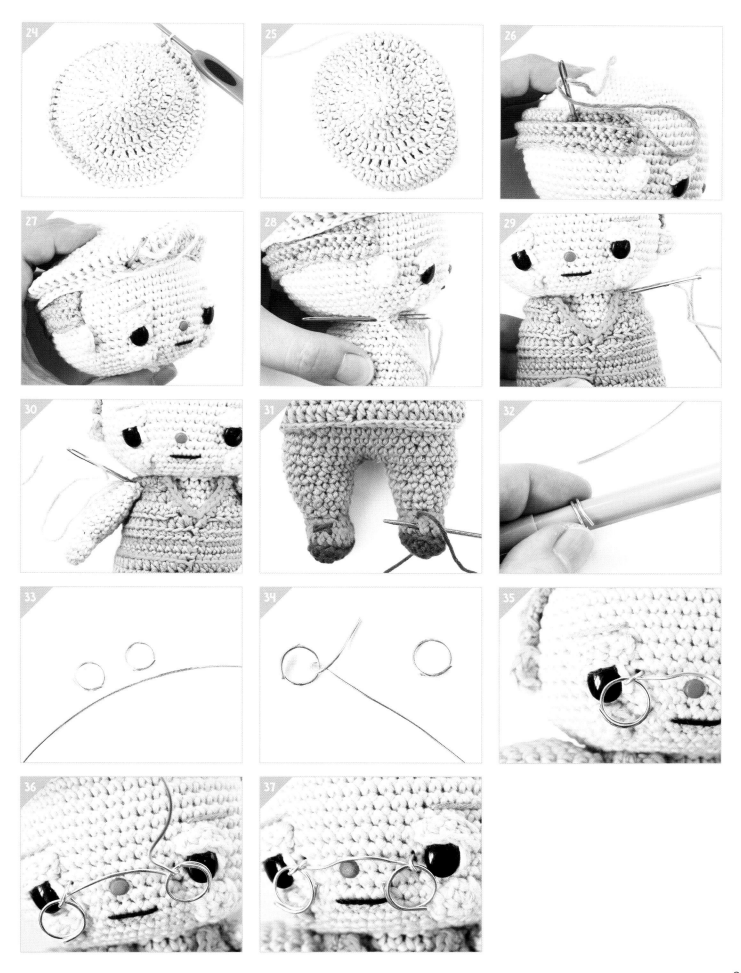

GRANDMA

HAIR

Large Hair Piece

Round 1: With Color C and Hair hook, make a magic ring, 6 sc in ring. (6 sc)

Round 2: Inc in each st around. (12 sc)

Round 3: [Sc in next st, inc in next st] 6 times. (18 sc)

Round 4: [Sc in next 2 sts, inc in next st] 6 times. (24 sc)

Round 5: [Sc in next 3 sts, inc in next st] 6 times. (30 sc)

Round 6: *(Hair Strands)* Sl st in next st, [ch 20, starting in 2nd ch from hook, hdc in each ch across (19 hdc); working in Round 5, skip next st, sl st in next st] 15 times. *(image 1)*

Fasten off, leaving a long tail for sewing.

Small Hair Piece

Round 1: With Color C and Hair hook, make a magic ring, 6 sc in ring. (6 sc)

Round 2: Inc in each st around. (12 sc)

Round 3: [Sc in next st, inc in next st] 6 times. (18 sc)

Round 4: [Sc in next 2 sts, inc in next st] 6 times. (24 sc)

Rounds 5-7: *(3 rounds)* Sc in each st around. (24 sc)

Round 8: *(Hair Strands)* Sl st in next st, [ch 20, starting in 2nd ch from hook, hdc in each ch across (19 hdc); working in Round 7, skip next st, sl st in next st] 12 times. *(image 2)*

Fasten off, leaving a long tail for sewing.

Attaching Hair

1. Position Large Hair Piece on Head, with wrong side up, so that the Hair Strands fall naturally over the Head. Sew around the crown to secure. *(image 3 & 4)*

2. Place Small Hair Piece on top of Large Hair Piece, with right side up. Stuff the "bun" and sew around the crown to secure. *(image 5)*

3. Adjust the Hair Strands with your fingers, either smoothing them out or making them curlier.

LEGS & BODY

Note: *The Legs and Body are worked in one piece.*

First Leg

Round 1: With Color J, ch 6; starting in 2nd ch from hook, sc in next 4 ch, 3 sc in last ch, working on other side of starting chain, sc in next 4 ch. (11 sc)

Round 2: Inc in first st, sc in next 4 sts, inc in each of next 2 sts, sc in next 3 sts, inc in the last st. (15 sc)

Round 3: Working in **back loops** only, sc in each st around. (15 sc)

Round 4: Sc in next 4 sts, [inv-dec] 4 times, sc in next 3 sts. (11 sc)

Change to MC.

Round 5: Working in **back loops** only, sc in next 3 sts, [inv-dec] 2 times, sc in next 4 sts. (9 sc)

Round 6: [Sc in next 2 sts, inc in next st] 3 times. (12 sc)

Rounds 7-9: *(3 rounds)* Sc in each st around. (12 sc)

Change to Color K.

Round 10: Sc in each st around. (12 sc)

Fasten off.

Stuff leg firmly.

Second Leg

Repeat instructions for First Leg but do not fasten off.

Body

Round 1: *(Joining Legs)* Working on Second Leg, ch 3; working on First Leg, with foot facing forward, sc in st at inside Leg, sc in next 11 sts; working in ch-3, sc in next 3 ch, working on Second Leg, sc in next 12 sts; working in unused loops on other side of ch-3, sc in next 3 ch; working on First Leg, sc in next 7 sts. *(image 6 & 7)*

Mark last st worked as new end of round.

Rounds 2-8: *(7 rounds)* Sc in each st around. (30 sc)

Change to Color J.

Round 9: Sc in each st around. (30 sc)

Round 10: Working in **back loops** only, sc in each st around. (30 sc)

Rounds 11-16: *(6 rounds)* Sc in each st around. (30 sc)

Round 17: [Sc in next 3 sts, inv-dec] 6 times. (24 sc)

Fasten off, leaving a long tail for sewing. *(image 8)*

Stuff Body firmly.

SKIRT

Note: *Round 1 is worked in the unused front loops of Round 9 on Body.*

Round 1: Holding Body upside down, join Color J with standing sc to any st at center back, sc in next 29 sts; join with sl st to first sc. (30 sc) *(image 9)*

Round 2: Ch 2, [dc in next 9 sts, 2 dc in next st] 3 times; join with sl st to first dc. (33 dc) *(image 10)*

Round 3: Ch 2, [dc in next 10 sts, 2 dc in next st] 3 times; join with sl st to first dc. (36 dc)

Rounds 4-5: *(2 rounds)* Ch 2, dc in each st around; join with sl st to first dc. (36 dc)

Change to Color K.

Round 6: Ch 1, working in **back loops** only, sl st in each st around. (36 sl sts) *(image 11)*

Fasten off and weave in ends.

Cardigan

Note: *Round 1 is worked around Round 17 of Body using Surface Single Crochet.*

Row 1: Holding Body upside down, join Color G with standing sc to st at center front, sc in next 24 sts (the first and last st overlap). Do not join. (25 sc) *(image 12 & 13)*

Work continues in Rows.

Row 2: Ch 2, turn, dc in first st, 2 dc in next st, [dc in next st, 2 dc in next st] 11 times, dc in last st. (37 dc) *(image 14)*

Rows 3-7: (5 rows) Ch 2, turn, dc in each st across. (37 dc) *(image 15)*

Edging: Sc in same st as last dc, working in sides of rows, [2 sc in next row, sc in next row] 3 times, sc in first row; working on other side; (sl st, sc) in first row, [2 sc in next row, sc in next row] 3 times, ending with sc in first dc on Row 7. *(image 16)*

Fasten off and weave in ends.

Granny Square Pocket

Round 1: With Yellow Floss and Appliqué hook, make a magic ring, 8 sc in ring; join with sl st to first sc. (8 sc) Fasten off.

Round 2: Join Ecru Floss with sl st to any st on Round 1, ch 3, 2dc-cl in same st, ch 2, [3dc-cl in next st, ch 2] 7 times; join with sl st to 3rd ch of beg ch-3. (8 petals) Fasten off. *(image 17 & 18)*

Round 3: Join Sea Green Floss with sl st to any ch-2 sp, ch 3, (dc, ch 2, 2 dc) in same sp, 2 hdc in next ch-2 sp, *(2 dc, ch 2, 2dc) in next sp, 2 hdc in next sp; repeat from * 2 times more; join with sl st to 3rd ch of beg ch-3. *(image 19 & 20)*

Fasten off, leaving a long tail for sewing.

ARM (Make 2)

Round 1: With MC, make a magic ring, 6 sc in ring. (6 sc)

Round 2: Inc in each st around. (12 sc)

Rounds 3-4: *(2 rounds)* Sc in each st around. (12 sc)

Round 5: [Inv-dec] 3 times, sc in the next 6 sts. (9 sc)

Rounds 6-12: *(7 rounds)* Sc in each st around. (9 sc)

Change to Color G.

Round 13: Sc in each st around. (9 sc)

Fasten off, leaving a long tail for sewing.

Stuff Arms lightly.

Sleeves

Note: *Round 1 is worked around Round 13 of each Arm using Surface Single Crochet.*

Round 1: Holding Arm upside down, join Color G with standing sc to any st on Round 13, sc in next 9 sts. (10 sc) *(image 21)*

Round 2: Ch 2, [dc in next 2 sts, 2 dc] 3 times, dc in last st; join with sl st to first dc. (13 dc)

Rounds 3-6: *(4 rounds)* Ch 2, dc in each st around; join with sl st to first dc. (13 dc)

Round 7: Ch 1, sc in each st around; join with sl st to first sc. (13 sc) *(image 22)*

Fasten off and weave in ends.

Repeat on other Arm.

FINAL DOLL ASSEMBLY

1. Sew Body to finished Head, adding more stuffing before finishing. *(image 23)*

2. Position the Arms and sew in place. *(image 24)*

3. With Color E and yarn needle, embroider a "V" on top of each shoe (for ribbon design). *(image 25)*

4. Sew the Granny Square Pocket on the Cardigan. *(image 26)*

5. Make Eye Glasses: Repeat instructions for Grandpa's Eye Glasses. *(image 27 & 28)*

6. Sew a mini Bead on each Ear for the Earrings. *(image 29)*

7. Sew 2 mini Beads on the front of Cardigan (for buttons). *(image 30)*

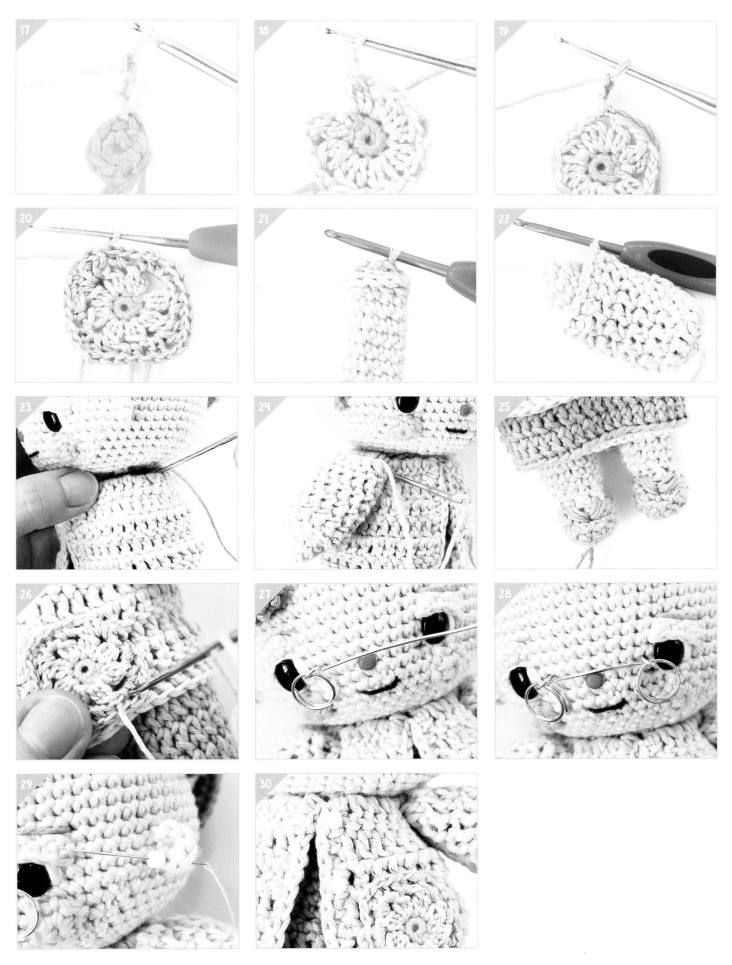

Elise & Isobel
Best Friends

These two BFFs go everywhere together on many a curious adventure. Elise is thoughtful and quiet and mostly calm; Isobel is full of energy and wiggles about constantly. Their contrasting characters almost always gets them into double the trouble!

MATERIALS & TOOLS

HELLO Cotton Yarn

Elise

» **Main Color (MC):** Powder Peach (163) - for Head, Arms & Legs
» **Color A:** White (154) - for Eye Whites, Shirt & Shoe Soles
» **Color B:** Light Pink (102) - for Cheeks
» **Color C:** Turquoise (134) - for Hair
» **Color D:** Light Yellow (122) - for Overalls
» **Color E:** Robin's Egg Blue (151) - for Stripes on Shirt
» **Color F:** Cherry Red (113) - for Shoes
» **Color G:** Off-White (155) - for Panda Hat
» **Color H:** Black (160) - for Panda Eyes & Ears on Hat
» **Color I:** Dark Grey (176) - for Braided Ties on Hat

Isobel

» **Main Color (MC):** Powder Peach (163) - for Head & Arms
» **Color A:** White (154) - for Eye Whites, Tights & Shirt
» **Color B:** Light Pink (102) - for Cheeks
» **Color D:** Light Yellow (122) - for Boots
» **Color J:** Mandarin Orange (115) - for Hair
» **Color K:** Green (133) - for Froggy Hood & Pinafore
» **Color L:** Lime Green (131) - for Stripes on Shirt
» **Color M:** Coral (111) - for Bow Tie & Boot Laces

Hook Sizes

» 3mm hook
» 3.5mm hook – for Hair, Hat & Hood

Other

» Stitch markers
» Yarn needle
» Stuffing
» Craft Glue
» Pins

For Each Doll

» Safety Eyes - Black Oval 3/8" (10mm) x 2
» Scrapbooking Brad - Orange 5/32" (4mm) x 1 - for Nose
» DMC Embroidery Floss - Black
» Embroidery needle
» Mini buttons x 2 - for Clothes
» Sewing needle & thread (to sew on buttons)

For Isobel

» Cartoon Safety Eyes - Black Oval ¼" (7mm) x 2

FINISHED SIZE
Each Doll is about 6½" (16.5cm) tall

SKILL LEVEL
Intermediate

PATTERN NOTES

The smaller size hook is used throughout, unless otherwise stated.

When working double crochet rows or rounds, the first ch-2 does not count as the first stitch. The first dc of a row is worked in the last stitch made on the previous row. The first dc of a round is worked in the same stitch as the previous round's join.

SPECIAL STITCHES

Surface Single Crochet (refer to Tips & Techniques): With right side of crochet piece facing, work between the stitches. Start with a slip knot on the hook and insert it in specified stitch and out in next stitch; pull up a loop (2 loops on hook); yarn over hook and draw through both loops on hook. (standing surface single crochet made)

For following stitches, insert hook in stitch where the hook came out of and out again in next stitch; pull up a loop (2 loops on hook); yarn over and draw through both loops. (Surface single crochet made)

Double Crochet Decrease (dc2tog) (refer to Special Stitches): Yarn over, insert hook in specified stitch or space and pull up a loop. Yarn over and draw through 2 loops on the hook. (2 loops remain) Yarn over, insert hook in next stitch or space and pull up a loop. Yarn over and draw through 2 loops on the hook. (3 loops remain) Yarn over and draw through all 3 loops on hook. (Double crochet decrease made)

ELISE & ISOBEL

HEAD

Round 1: With MC, make a magic ring, 6 sc in ring. (6 sc)

Round 2: Inc in each st around. (12 sc)

Round 3: [Sc in next st, inc in next st] 6 times. (18 sc)

Round 4: [Sc in next 2 sts, inc in next st] 6 times. (24 sc)

Round 5: [Sc in next 3 sts, inc in next st] 6 times. (30 sc)

Round 6: [Sc in next 4 sts, inc in next st] 6 times. (36 sc)

Round 7: [Sc in next 5 sts, inc in next st] 6 times. (42 sc)

Round 8: [Sc in next 6 sts, inc in next st] 6 times. (48 sc)

Round 9: [Sc in next 7 sts, inc in next st] 6 times. (54 sc)

Round 10: [Sc in next 8 sts, inc in next st] 6 times. (60 sc)

Rounds 11-21: *(11 rounds)* Sc in each st around. (60 sc)

Round 22: [Sc in next 8 sts, inv-dec] 6 times. (54 sc) *(image 1)*

Round 23: [Sc in next 7 sts, inv-dec] 6 times. (48 sc)

Round 24: [Sc in next 6 sts, inv-dec] 6 times. (42 sc)

Add Facial Features:

1. Nose - position brad at front of Head (about 27th stitch on Round 20) and lock in place. *(image 2 & 3)*

2. Eyes - position on Round 19, about 6 stitches from either side of Nose and secure in place. *(image 4 & 5)*

3. Eye Whites - using Color A and yarn needle, make 3-4 vertical straight stitches (the same height as Eyes) to the left of each Eye. Knot and secure the yarn on the inside of the Head. *(image 6)*

Continue crocheting:

Round 25: [Sc in next 5 sts, inv-dec] 6 times. (36 sc)

Round 26: [Sc in next 4 sts, inv-dec] 6 times. (30 sc)

Round 27: [Sc in next 3 sts, inv-dec] 6 times. (24 sc)

Start stuffing Head, adding more as you go.

Round 28: [Sc in next 2 sts, inv-dec] 6 times. (18 sc)

Round 29: [Sc in next st, inv-dec] 6 times. (12 sc)

Round 30: [Inv dec] 6 times. (6 sc) Fasten off.

Close the opening securely and leave a long tail (for Eye Indentations). *(image 7)*

Cheek (Make 2)

Round 1: With Color B, make a magic ring, 6 sc in ring. (6 sc)

Fasten off with Needle Join, leaving a long tail for sewing.

FINISHING THE FACE

Eye Indentations

Using long tail on Head and yarn needle:

1. Bring needle up from base of Head and out next to the nose-side of Eye. *(image 8)*

2. Insert needle in next stitch, bringing it out at base of Head. Gently tug yarn to create a slight indentation at the Eye. *(image 9)*

3. Repeat steps 1 & 2 for other Eye. *(image 10 & 11)*

4. Secure yarn tail with a knot at base of Head and trim excess yarn.

Cheeks - Position the Cheeks below each Eye and sew in place, bringing the yarn out at base of Head. Secure with a knot and trim excess yarn. *(image 12)*

Eyebrows & Mouth

Using Black Embroidery Floss and needle:

1. Bring needle up from base of Head and embroider Eyebrows above each Eye – by making a diagonal straight stitch from Round 16 to Round 17, about 4 stitches long. *(image 13)*

2. After Eyebrows, bring needle down through Head to create a Mouth on Round 22, centered under the Nose – by making a loose horizontal straight stitch, about 3 stitches long, bringing needle out at base of Head. Tie ends in a knot to secure and trim excess yarn. *(image 14)*

3. Optional: Apply glue on Mouth, and use pins to shape the smile while the glue dries. *(image 15 & 16)*

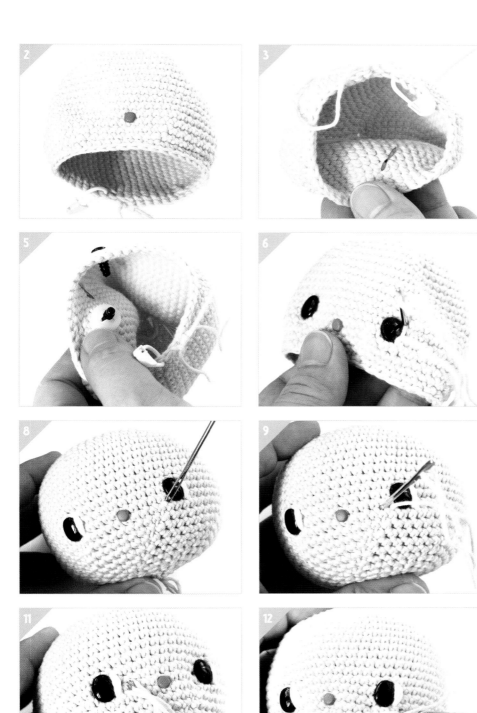
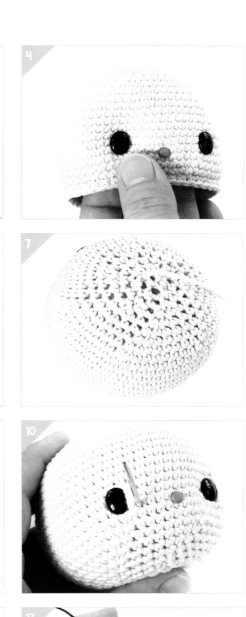

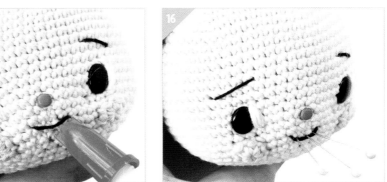

HAIR

Round 1: With Color C and larger hook, make a magic ring, ch 2, 10 dc in ring; join with sl st to first dc. (10 dc)

Round 2: Ch 2, 2 dc in each st around; join with sl st to first dc. (20 dc)

Round 3: Ch 2, [dc in next st, 2 dc in next st] around; join with sl st to first dc. (30 dc)

Round 4: Ch 2, [dc in next 2 sts, 2 dc in next st] around; join with sl st to first dc. (40 dc)

Round 5: Ch 2, [dc in next 3 sts, 2 dc in next st] around; join with sl st to first dc. (50 dc)

Round 6: Ch 2, dc in each st around; join with sl st to first dc. (50 dc)

Round 7: Ch 2, dc in each st around; sl st in base of first st (same st as previous round's join). (50 dc & 1 sl st)

Work continues in Rows.

Row 1: Ch 2, turn, skip sl st, dc in next 50 sts, sl st in base of beg ch-2 (same st on Round 7). (50 dc & 1 sl st) *(image 17)*

Fasten off with Needle Join, leaving a long tail for sewing.

Pigtails (Make 2)

Round 1: With Color C, make a magic ring, 6 sc in ring. (6 sc)

Round 2: Sc in each st around. (6 sc)

Round 3: [Sc in next st, inc in next st] around. (9 sc)

Round 4: Sc in each st around. (9 sc)

Round 5: [Sc in next 2 sts, inc in next st] around. (12 sc)

Round 6: Sc in each st around. (12 sc)

Fasten off, leaving a long tail for sewing.

Flatten piece.

Attaching Hair

1. Position the Hair on the Head, creating a "side parting", and sew in place. *(image 18)*

2. Using long tail and yarn needle, whipstitch last round of Pigtails closed, then thread tail inside piece and out through magic ring. *(image 19)*

3. Position Pigtails on either side of Head, with Round 1's point on Row 1 of Hair, and using long tail, sew only the point of the Pigtail in place. *(image 20)*

LEGS & BODY

Note: *The Legs and Body are worked in one piece.*

First Leg

Round 1: With Color A, ch 6; starting in 2nd ch from hook, sc in next 4 ch, 3 sc in last ch, working on other side of starting chain, sc in next 4 ch. (11 sc)

Round 2: Inc in first st, sc in next 4 sts, inc in each of next 2 sts, sc in next 3 sts, inc in last st. (15 sc)

Change to Color F.

Round 3: Working in **back loops** only, sc in each st around. (15 sc)

Round 4: Sc in next 4 sts, [inv-dec] 4 times, sc in next 3 sts. (11 sc)

Round 5: Sc in next 3 sts, [inv-dec] 2 times, sc in next 4 sts. (9 sc)

Change to MC.

Rounds 6-8: (3 rounds) Sc in each st around. (9 sc)

Change to Color D.

Round 9: Sc in each st around. (9 sc) *(image 21)*

Fasten off. Stuff Leg firmly.

Second Leg

Repeat instructions for First Leg but do not fasten off.

Body

Joining Round: Working on Second Leg, ch 3; working on First Leg, with foot facing forward, sc in st at inside Leg, sc in next 8 sts; working in ch-3, sc in next 3 ch; working on Second Leg, sc in next 9 sts; working in unused loops on other side of ch-3, sc in next 3 ch; working on First Leg, sc in next 6 sts. *(image 22 & 23)*

Mark last st worked as new end of round.

Round 2: [Inc in next st, sc in next 3 sts] 6 times. (30 sc)

Rounds 3-7: (5 rounds) Sc in each st around. (30 sc)

Round 8: Sc in next 3 sts, change to Color A, working in **back loops** only, sc in next 27 sts. (30 sc)

Rounds 9-12: (4 rounds) Sc in each st around. (30 sc)

Round 13: [Sc in next 3 sts, inv-dec] around. (24 sc)

Fasten off, leaving a long tail for sewing. *(image 24)*

Stuff Body firmly.

Pants Cuffs

Note: *Round 1 is worked around Round 9 on each Leg using Surface Single Crochet.*

Round 1: Holding Legs upside down, join Color D with standing sc to any st on Round 9, sc in next 9 sts; join with sl st to first sc. (10 sc) *(image 25)*

Fasten off and weave in ends.

Repeat on other Leg.

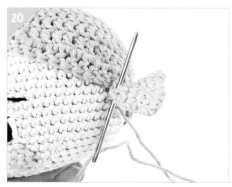

Shirt Stripes

With Color E and yarn needle, embroider small back stitches around the Body on Rounds 8-13. *(image 26)*

Overall Strap (Make 2)

Row 1: With Color D, ch 25, starting in 2nd ch from hook, sc in each ch across. (24 sc)

Fasten off, leaving a long tail for sewing.

ARM (Make 2)

Round 1: With MC, make a magic ring, 7 sc in ring. (7 sc)

Rounds 2-7: *(6 rounds)* Sc in each st around. (7 sc)

Change to Color A.

Rounds 8-10: *(3 rounds)* Sc in each st around. (7 sc)

Fasten off, leaving a long tail for sewing.

Stuff Arm lightly.

Arm Stripes

With Color E and yarn needle, embroider small backstitches around Arm on Rounds 8-10.

PANDA HAT

Rounds 1: With Color G and Hat hook, repeat Rounds 1-5 of the Hair.

Rounds 6-8: *(3 rounds)* Ch 2, dc in each st around; join with sl st to first dc. (50 dc)

At the end of Round 8, do not fasten off.

First Earflap

Row 1: Ch 2, dc in first st, dc in next 4 sts. (5 dc)

Leave remaining sts unworked.

Row 2: Ch 2, turn, dc2tog (using first 2 sts), dc in next st, dc2tog (using last 2 sts) (3 dc)

Row 3: Ch 2, turn, dc2tog (using first 2 sts), dc in last st. (2 dc)

Row 4: Ch 2, turn, dc2tog (1 dc) *(image 27)*

Fasten off, leaving a long tail (for braids).

Second Earflap

Place Hat on Head, positioning the First Earflap in front of one Pigtail. From the other Pigtail, on Round 8 of Hat, mark 5 stitches in.

Row 1: With right side facing, using Color G and Hat hook, join yarn with sl st to marked st on Round 8, ch 2, dc in same st as joining, dc in next 4 sts. (5 dc)

Rows 2-4: Repeat Rows 2-4 of First Earflap. *(image 28)*

Fasten off, leaving a long tail (for braids).

Panda Eye (Make 2)

With Color H, ch 5; starting in 2nd ch from hook, sc in next 3 ch, 3 sc in last ch, working on other side of starting

chain, sc in next 2 ch, inc in last ch (10 sc)

Fasten off with Needle Join, leaving a long tail for sewing.

Panda Ear (Make 2)

Round 1: With Color H, make a magic ring, 6 sc in ring. (6 sc)

Round 2: Inc in each st around. (12 sc)

Rounds 3-5: *(3 rounds)* Sc in each st around. (12 sc)

Fasten off, leaving a long tail for sewing.

Do not stuff. Flatten Ear.

Assembling the Hat

1. Position the Eyes (at a slant) between Rounds 6 & 8 on front of Hat. Sewn in place.

2. Using Color H and yarn needle, embroider 8 horizontal straight stitches, 2-stitches long, for a Nose.

3. Embroider an upside down "V" for the mouth. *(image 29)*

4. Using Color B and yarn needle, embroider Cheeks.

5. Position the Ears on Round 3, with 5-6 stitches in between, and sew in place. *(image 30)*

6. Braids – Cut 10" (25cm) long strands – 4 of Color G & 2 of Color I.

a. Using 2 strands Color G & 1 strand Color I, thread strands through point of Earflap. *(image 31)*

b. Using long tail and strands, braid together. With a separate yarn strand, fasten the end of braid with a double knot. Trim the yarn ends. *(image 32)*

c. Repeat steps a & b on other Earflap, to match first Braid.

FINAL DOLL ASSEMBLY

1. Sew Body to finished Head, adding more stuffing before finishing. *(image 33)*

2. Position Arms and sew in place. *(image 34)*

3. Pin Overall Straps in place, crossing them at the back. Sew to secure. *(image 35 & 36)*

4. Sew buttons to front of each Strap. *(image 37)*

5. With Color A and yarn needle, embroider "shoelaces" - making 2 horizontal stitches, 2-stitches long - on front of each Shoe. *(image 38)*

6. Place Hat on Head. *(image 39)*

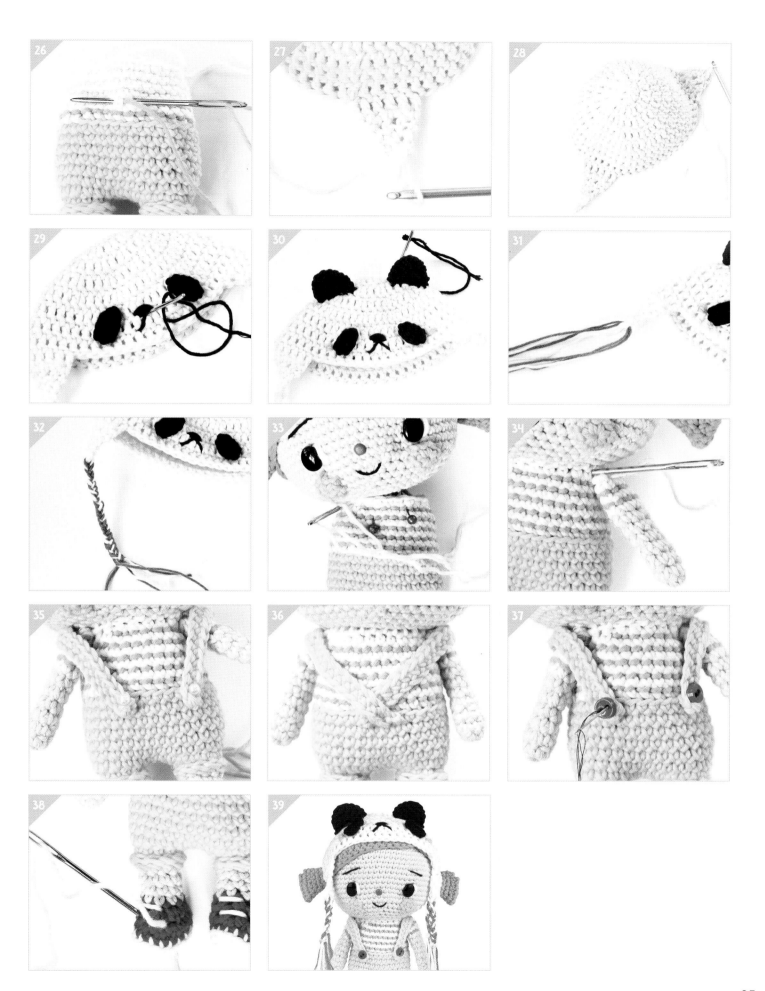

HAIR

Row 1: With Color J, ch 10, starting in 2nd ch from hook, sc in each st across. (9 sc)

Rows 2-20: *(19 rows)* Ch 1, turn, working in **back loops** only, sc in each st across. (9 sc) *(image 1)*

Fasten off, leaving a long tail for sewing.

Attaching Hair

Position Hair on Head (slightly slanted, with one side directly above right Eyebrow), and sew in place. *(image 2)*

HOOD

Rounds 1-10: With Color K and Hood hook, repeat Rounds 1-10 of Head.

Rounds 11-23: *(13 rounds)* Sc in each st around. (60 sc)

Place Head into Hood before continuing.

Round 24: [Sc in next 8 sts, inv-dec] 6 times. (54 sc) *(image 3)*

Round 25: [Sc in next 7 sts, inv-dec] 6 times. (48 sc)

Fasten off, leaving a long tail for sewing.

Using long tail and yarn needle, sew Hood securely to Head using small backstitches.

Frog Eye (Make 2)

Round 1: With Color K, make a magic ring, 6 sc in ring. (6 sc)

Round 2: Inc in each st around. (12 sc)

Rounds 3-5: *(3 rounds)* Sc in each st around. (12 sc)

Fasten off, leaving a long tail for sewing.

Do not stuff. Flatten piece.

Insert and secure Cartoon Safety Eyes.

Finishing the Hood

1. Position Frog Eyes on top of Head, at about Round 19 of Hood, and sew in place. *(image 4)*

2. With Black Floss, embroider a smile for the Frog, centered between Frog Eyes, on Round 22 of Hood.

3. Using Color B, embroider Cheeks on Frog. *(image 5)*

LEGS & BODY

Note: *The Legs and Body are worked in one piece.*

First Leg

Round 1: With Color D, ch 6; starting in 2nd ch from hook, sc in next 4 ch, 3 sc in last ch, working on other side of starting chain, sc in next 4 ch. (11 sc)

Round 2: Inc in first st, sc in next 4 sts, inc in each of next 2 sts, sc in next 3 sts, inc in last st. (15 sc)

Round 3: Working in **back loops** only, sc in each st around. (15 sc)

Round 4: Sc in next 4 sts, [inv-dec] 4 times, sc in next 3 sts. (11 sc)

Round 5: Sc in next 3 sts, [inv-dec] 2 times, sc in next 4 sts. (9 sc)

Rounds 6-7: *(2 rounds)* Sc in each st around. (9 sc)

Change to Color A.

Rounds 8-9: *(2 rounds)* Sc in each st around. (9 sc)

Fasten off. *(image 6)*

Stuff Leg firmly.

Second Leg

Repeat instructions for First Leg but do not fasten off.

Body

Joining Round: Working on Second Leg, ch 3; working on First Leg, with foot facing forward, sc in st at inside Leg, sc in next 8 sts; working in ch-3, sc in next 3 ch; working on Second Leg, sc in next 9 sts; working in unused loops on other side of ch-3, sc in next 3 ch; working on First Leg, sc in next 6 sts. *(image 7 & 8)*

Mark last st worked as new end of round.

Round 2: [Inc in next st, sc in next 3 sts] 6 times. (30 sc)

Rounds 3-5: *(3 rounds)* Sc in each st around. (30 sc)

Change to Color K.

Round 6: Sc in each st around. (30 sc)

Round 7: Working in **back loops** only, sc in each st around. (30 sc)

Change to Color A.

Round 8: Sc in each st around. (30 sc)

Change to Color L.

Rounds 9-10: *(2 rounds)* Sc in each st around. (30 sc)

Change to Color A.

Round 11: Sc in each st around. (30 sc)

Change to Color L.

Rounds 12-13: *(2 rounds)* Sc in each st around. (30 sc)

Change to Color A.

Round 14: [Sc in next 3 sts, inv-dec] around. (24 sc)

Fasten off, leaving a long tail for sewing. *(image 9)*

Stuff Body firmly.

Boot Cuffs

Note: *Round 1 is worked around Round 7 on each Leg using Surface Single Crochet.*

Round 1: Holding Legs upside down, join Color D with standing sc to any st on Round 7, sc in next 9 sts; join with sl st to first sc. (10 sc) *(image 10)*

Fasten off and weave in ends.

Repeat on other Leg.

Pinafore Skirt

Note: *Round 1 is worked in the unused front loops of Round 6 on Body.*

Round 1: Holding Body upside down, join Color K with standing sc to st at center back, sc in same st , [inc in next st] around; join with sl st to first sc. (60 sc) *(image 11 & 12)*

Rounds 2-4: *(3 rounds)* Ch 1, sc in each st around; join with sl st to first sc. (60 sc) *(image 13)*

Fasten off and weave in ends.

Skirt Strap (Make 2)

Row 1: With Color K, ch 25, starting in 2nd ch from hook, sc in each st across. (24 sc)

Fasten off, leaving a long tail for sewing.

Bowtie

Row 1: With Color M, ch 8, starting in 2nd ch from hook, sc in each st across. (7 sc)

Row 2: Ch 1, turn, sc in each st across. (7 sc)

Fasten off, leaving a long tail for sewing. *(image 14)*

Twist the ends of Bowtie to form the shape. Wrap the tail about 3 times around the center and secure. *(image 15 & 16)*

FINAL DOLL ASSEMBLY

1. Sew Body to finished Head (working through the Hood into the Head), adding more stuffing before finishing. Make sure the Body is securely attached. *(image 17, 18 & 19)*

2. Position Arms and sew in place. *(image 20)*

3. Pin Skirt Straps in place, crossing them at the back. Sew to secure. *(image 21 & 22)*

4. Sew on Bowtie. *(image 23)*

5. Sew buttons to front of each Strap. *(image 24)*

6. With Color M and yarn needle, embroider 2 "X"s to the front of each Boot as "shoelaces". *(image 25)*

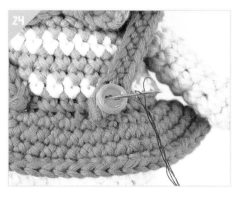

MOMMY and TWINS
Josh & Jake

Mommy always thinks she can handle the twins on her own, but boy, she is wrong, time and time again! Summer is the family's favorite time of the year, but also when Mommy is the most tired (from running after the boys at the beach!)

MATERIALS & TOOLS

HELLO Cotton Yarn

Mommy

» **Main Color (MC):** Powder Peach (163) - for Head, Body, Arms & Legs
» **Color A:** White (154) - for Eye Whites
» **Color B1:** Light Pink (102) - for Cheeks
» **Color C:** Blue (148) - for Hair
» **Color D:** Mint Green (138) for Swimsuit & Sandal Soles
» **Color E:** Coral (111) - for Flowers and Sandals
» **Color F:** Off-White (155) - for Beach Tunic
» **Color G:** Mocha (125) - for Hat

Josh

» **Main Color (MC):** Powder Peach (163) - for Head, Ears & Arms
» **Color A:** White (154) - for Eye Whites
» **Color B2:** Baby Pink (101) - for Cheeks
» **Color C:** Blue (148) - for Hair
» **Color H:** Turquoise (134) - for Body Suit
» **Color I:** Royal Blue (150) - for Pattern on Body Suit
» **Color J:** Bright Orange (118) - for Flippers
» **Color K:** Kelly Green (132) - for Snorkeling Mask
» **Color L:** Light Gray (175) - for Snorkeling Mask
» **Color M:** Light Yellow (122) - for Snorkel

Jake

» **Main Color (MC):** Powder Peach (163) - for Head, Ears, Arms & Legs
» **Color A:** White (154) - for Eye Whites
» **Color B2:** Baby Pink (101) - for Cheeks

» **Color C:** Blue (148) - for Hair
» **Color F:** Off-White (155) - for Shirt
» **Color H:** Turquoise (134) - for Pants
» **Color I:** Royal Blue (150) - for Sandals
» **Color J:** Bright Orange (118) - for Sandal Soles & Lion Mane
» **Color M:** Light Yellow (122) - for Swim Ring
» **Color N:** Brown (126) - Lion Eyes & Nose

Hook Sizes

» 2mm – for Floss Applique
» 3mm hook – Main hook
» 3.5mm hook– for Twins' Hair
» 4mm hook– for Tunic
» 5mm hook – for Mommy's Hat

Other
For Each Doll:

» Stitch markers
» Yarn needle
» Stuffing
» Craft Glue
» Pins
» Safety Eyes - Black Oval 3/8" (10mm) x 2
» Scrapbooking Brad - Orange 5/32" (4mm) x 1 - for Nose
» DMC Embroidery Floss - Black
» Embroidery Needle

For Jake:

» DMC Embroidery Floss - Dark Green, Dark Brown, Light Brown

FINISHED SIZE	SKILL LEVEL
Mommy - About 8" (20cm) tall	Intermediate
Each Twin - About 6¼" (16cm) tall	

PATTERN NOTES

The main size hook is used throughout, unless otherwise stated.

When working double crochet rows or rounds, the first ch-2 does not count as the first stitch. The first dc of a row is worked in the last stitch made on the previous row. The first dc of a round is worked in the same stitch as the previous round's join.

When working half-double crochet rows or rounds, the first ch-2 does not count as the first stitch. The first hdc of a row is worked in the last stitch made on the previous row. The first hdc of a round is worked in the same stitch as the previous round's join.

SPECIAL STITCHES

Half-Double Crochet Decrease (hdc2tog): Yarn over, insert hook in specified stitch or space and pull up a loop. (3 loops on hook) Yarn over, insert hook in next stitch or space and pull up a loop. (5 loops on hook) Yarn over and draw through all 5 loops on hook. (Half-double crochet decrease made)

Surface Single Crochet (refer to Tips & Techniques): With right side of crochet piece facing, work between the stitches. Start with a slip knot on the hook and insert it in specified stitch and out in next stitch; pull up a loop (2 loops on hook); yarn over hook and draw through both loops on hook. (Standing surface single crochet made) For following stitches, insert hook in stitch where the hook came out of and out again in next stitch; pull up a loop (2 loops on hook); yarn over and draw through both loops. (Surface single crochet made)

Treble Crochet (tr) (refer to Special Crochet Stitches): Yarn over hook twice, insert hook in stitch or space specified and pull up a loop (4 loops on hook), [yarn over and draw through 2 loops on hook] 3 times. Treble crochet stitch made.

MOMMY

HEAD

Round 1: With MC, make a magic ring, 6 sc in ring. (6 sc)

Round 2: Inc in each st around. (12 sc)

Round 3: [Sc in next st, inc in next st] 6 times. (18 sc)

Round 4: [Sc in next 2 sts, inc in next st] 6 times. (24 sc)

Round 5: [Sc in next 3 sts, inc in next st] 6 times. (30 sc)

Round 6: [Sc in next 4 sts, inc in next st] 6 times. (36 sc)

Round 7: [Sc in next 5 sts, inc in next st] 6 times. (42 sc)

Round 8: [Sc in next 6 sts, inc in next st] 6 times. (48 sc)

Round 9: [Sc in next 7 sts, inc in next st] 6 times. (54 sc)

Round 10: [Sc in next 8 sts, inc in next st] 6 times. (60 sc)

Rounds 11-21: *(11 rounds)* Sc in each st around. (60 sc)

Round 22: [Sc in next 8 sts, inv-dec] 6 times. (54 sc) *(image 1)*

Round 23: [Sc in next 7 sts, inv-dec] 6 times. (48 sc)

Round 24: [Sc in next 6 sts, inv-dec] 6 times. (42 sc)

Add Facial Features:

1. Nose - position brad at front of Head (about 27ᵗʰ stitch on Round 20) and lock in place. *(image 2 & 3)*

2. Eyes - position on Round 19, about 6 stitches from either side of Nose and secure in place. *(image 4 & 5)*

3. Eye Whites - using Color A and yarn needle, make 3-4 vertical straight stitches (the same height as Eyes) to the

left of each Eye. Knot and secure the yarn on the inside of the Head. *(image 6)*

Continue crocheting:

Round 25: [Sc in next 5 sts, inv-dec] 6 times. (36 sc)

Round 26: [Sc in next 4 sts, inv-dec] 6 times. (30 sc)

Round 27: [Sc in next 3 sts, inv-dec] 6 times. (24 sc)

Start stuffing Head, adding more as you go.

Round 28: [Sc in next 2 sts, inv-dec] 6 times. (18 sc)

Round 29: [Sc in next st, inv-dec] 6 times. (12 sc)

Round 30: [Inv dec] 6 times. (6 sc)

Fasten off.

Close the opening securely and leave a long tail (for Eye Indentations). *(image 7)*

Cheek (Make 2)

Round 1: With Color B1, make a magic ring, 6 sc in ring. (6 sc)

Fasten off with Needle Join, leaving a long tail for sewing.

FINISHING THE FACE

Eye Indentations

Using long tail on Head and yarn needle:

1. Bring needle up from base of Head and out next to the nose-side of Eye. *(image 8)*

2. Insert needle in next stitch, bringing it out at base of Head. Gently tug yarn to create a slight indentation at the Eye. *(image 9)*

3. Repeat steps 1 & 2 for other Eye. *(image 10 & 11)*

4. Secure yarn tail with a knot at base of Head and trim excess yarn.

Cheeks - Position the Cheeks below each Eye and sew in place, bringing the yarn out at base of Head. Secure with a knot and trim excess yarn. *(image 12)*

Eyebrows & Mouth

Using Black Embroidery Floss and needle:

1. Bring needle up from base of Head and embroider Eyebrows above each Eye – by making a diagonal straight stitch from Round 16 to Round 17, about 4 stitches long. *(image 13)*

2. After Eyebrows, bring needle down through Head to create a Mouth on Round 22, centered under the Nose – by making a loose horizontal straight stitch, about 4 stitches long, bringing needle out at base of Head. Tie ends in a knot to secure and trim excess yarn. *(image 14)*

3. Optional: Apply glue on Mouth, and use pins to shape the smile while the glue dries. *(image 15 & 16)*

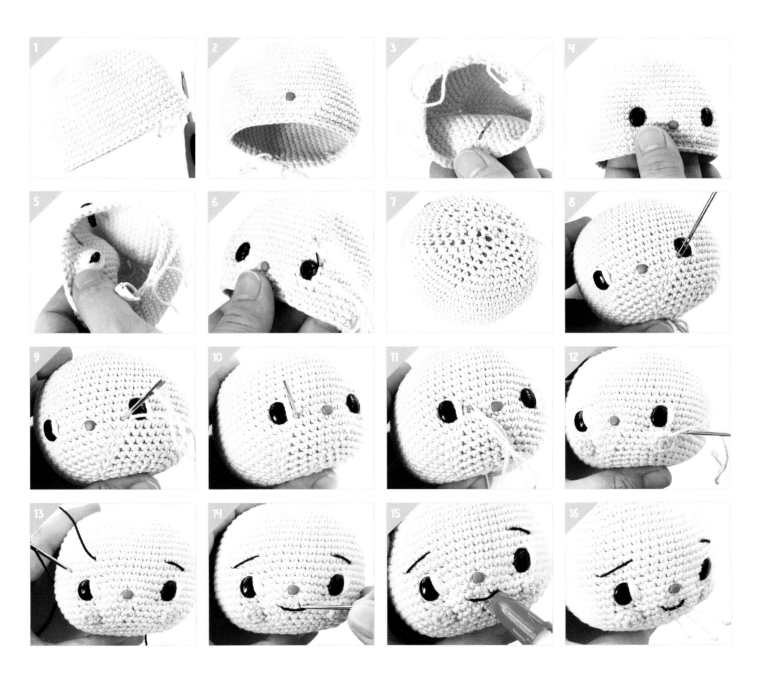

HAIR

Row 1: With Color C, ch 30, starting in 2nd ch from hook, dc in each st across. (29 dc)

Rows 2-21: (20 rows) Ch 2, turn, working in **back loops** only, dc in each st across. (29 dc)

Row 22: Ch 2, turn, working in **back loops** only, dc in first st, dc in next 13 sts. (14 dc) Leave remaining sts unworked.

Rows 23-29: (7 rows) Ch 2, turn, working in **back loops** only, dc in each st across (14 dc)

Fasten off, leaving a long tail for sewing.

Finishing and Attaching Hair

1. Whipstitch the edges of Row 29 to Row 1, matching stitches. *(image 17)*

2. With a new strand of Color C, sew running stitches around top opening of Hair. Pull tightly to close. Sew several stitches to secure the shape. *(image 18 & 19)*

3. Place Hair on Head and sew in place, leaving the longer end flowing. *(image 20)*

BODY

Rounds 1-6: Using Color D, repeat Rounds 1-6 of Head.

Rounds 7-20: *(14 rounds)* Sc in each st around. (36 sc)

Change to MC.

Round 21: Working in **back loops** only, [sc in next 4 sts, inv-dec] 6 times. (30 sc)

Round 22: [Sc in next 3 sts, inv-dec] 6 times. (24 sc)

Fasten off, leaving a long tail for sewing.

Stuff Body firmly. *(image 21)*

ARM (Make 2)

Round 1: With MC, make a magic ring, 6 sc in ring. (6 sc)

Round 2: Inc in each st around. (12 sc)

Rounds 3-4: *(2 rounds)* Sc in each st around. (12 sc)

Round 5: [Inv-dec] 3 times, sc in the next 6 sts. (9 sc)

Rounds 6-13: *(8 rounds)* Sc in each st around. (9 sc)

Fasten off, leaving a long tail for sewing.

Stuff Arm lightly. *(image 22)*

LEG - with Sandal (Make 2)

Round 1: With Color D, ch 8; starting in 2nd ch from hook, sc in next 6 ch, 3 sc in last ch, working on other side of starting chain, sc in next 6 ch. (15 sc)

Round 2: Inc in first st, sc in next 6 sts, inc in next 2 sts, sc in next 5 sts, inc in last st. (19 sc)

Change to MC.

Round 3: Working in **back loops** only, sc in each st around. (19 sc)

Round 4: Sc in each st around.

Round 5: Sc in next 8 sts, [inv-dec] 3 times, sc in next 5 sts. (16 sc)

Round 6: Sc in next 7 sts, [inv-dec] 4 times, sc in the last st. (12 sc)

Rounds 7-13: *(7 rounds)* Sc in each st around. (12 sc)

Fasten off, leaving a long tail for sewing. *(image 23)*

Stuff Leg firmly.

BEACH TUNIC

Back Panel

Row 1: (Right Side) With Color F and Tunic hook, ch 16, starting in 2nd ch from hook, sc in each ch across. (15 sc) *(image 24)*

Row 2: Ch 1, turn, hdc in first st, [ch 1, skip next st, hdc in next st] 7 times. (8 hdc & 7 ch-1 sps) *(image 25)*

Rows 3-10: (8 rows) Ch 1, turn, [hdc in next ch-sp, ch 1] 7 times, hdc in last st. (8 hdc & 7 ch-1 sps) *(image 26 & 27)*

Fasten off, leaving a long tail for sewing.

Side Panel (Make 2)

Row 1: (Right Side) With Color F and Tunic hook, ch 12, starting in 2nd ch from hook, sc in each ch across. (11 sc)

Row 2: Ch 1, turn, hdc in first st, [ch 1, skip next st, hdc in next st] 5 times. (6 hdc & 5 ch-1 sps)

Rows 3-10: *(8 rows)* Ch 1, turn, [hdc in ch-sp, ch 1] 5 times, hdc in last st. (6 hdc & 5 ch-1 sps)

Fasten off, leaving a long tail for sewing.

Belt

Row 1: With Color F and Main hook, ch 60.

Fasten off. Knot the ends and trim excess.

Beach Tunic Assembly

1. With right sides facing, whipstitch each Side Panel to Back Panel, leaving about ½″ (1.5cm) armhole on each side. *(image 28 & 29)*

2. Weave in ends neatly on wrong side of Tunic. *(image 30)*

3. With right side facing, join Color F (using Main hook) with standing sc to top corner of Tunic, sc evenly around, working 2 sc in each corner. Fasten off and weave in ends. *(image 31)*

HAT

Hint: *Use 2 separate balls of yarn – holding one strand from each.*

Rounds 1-8: With double strand of Color G and Hat hook, repeat Rounds 1-8 of Head.

Rounds 9-13: (5 rounds) Sc in each st around. (48 sc)

Round 14: Inc in each st around. (96 sc)

Round 15: Hdc in first st, [ch 4, skip next 2 sts, hdc in next st] 31 times, ch 4, skip next 2 sts; join with sl st to first hdc. *(image 32)*

Fasten off and weave in ends.

FINAL DOLL ASSEMBLY

1. Sew Body to finished Head, adding more stuffing before finishing. *(image 33)*

2. With Color E and yarn needle, embroider flowers on the front of the Body. *(image 34)*

3. Position Arms and sew in place. *(image 35)*

4. Position Legs and sew in place.*(image 36)*

5. With Color E and yarn needle, embroider straps on the feet (for Sandals). *(image 37 & 38)*

6. Slip Beach Tunic over Doll, and tie Belt around waist. *(image 39)*

7. Place Hat on Head. *(image 40)*

HEAD

Rounds 1-9: With MC, repeat Rounds 1-9 of Mommy's Head.

Rounds 10-19: *(10 rounds)* Sc in each st around. (54 sc)

Round 20: [Sc in next 7 sts, inv-dec] 6 times. (48 sc)

Round 21: [Sc in next 6 sts, inv-dec] 6 times. (42 sc)

Add Facial Features:

4. Nose - position brad at center of Head (about 25th stitch on Round 19) and lock in place. *(image 1)*

5. Eyes - position on Round 18, about 6 stitches from either side of Nose and secure in place. *(image 2 & 3)*

6. Eye Whites - using Color A and yarn needle, make 3-4 vertical straight stitches (the same height as Eyes) to the left of each Eye. Knot and secure the yarn on the inside of the Head. *(image 4)*

Continue crocheting:

Round 22: [Sc in next 5 sts, inv-dec] 6 times. (36 sc)

Round 23: [Sc in next 4 sts, inv-dec] 6 times. (30 sc)

Round 24: [Sc in next 3 sts, inv-dec] 6 times. (24 sc)

Round 25: [Sc in next 2 sts, inv-dec] 6 times. (18 sc)

Start stuffing Head, adding more as you go.

Round 26: [Sc in next st, inv-dec] 6 times. (12 sc)

Round 27: [Inv-dec] 6 times. (6 sc)

Fasten off and close the opening securely, leaving a long tail (to make the eye indentations). *(image 5)*

Cheek (Make 2)

Round 1: With Color B2, make a magic ring, 6 sc in ring. (6 sc)

Fasten off with Needle Join, leaving a long tail for sewing.

FINISHING THE FACE

Eye Indentations & Cheeks

Repeat instructions from Mommy's Head. *(images 6-11)*

Eyebrows

Using Black Embroidery Floss and needle:

Bring needle up from base of Head and embroider Eyebrows above each Eye – by making a diagonal straight stitch from Round 15 to Round 16, about 3 stitches long.

Mouth

Repeat instructions from Mommy's Head. Repeat instructions from Mommy's Head but position the mouth on Round 22. *(image 12)*

Ear (Make 2)

Round 1: With MC, make a magic ring, 6 sc in ring. (6 sc)

Fasten off, leaving a long tail for sewing.

HAIR

Round 1: With Color C and Twin's Hair hook, make a magic ring, ch 2, 10 hdc in ring; join with sl st to first hdc. (10 hdc)

Round 2: Ch 2, 2 hdc in each st around; join with sl st to first hdc. (20 hdc)

Round 3: Ch 2, [hdc in next st, 2 hdc in next st] around; join with sl st to first hdc. (30 hdc)

Round 4: Ch 2, [hdc in next 2 sts, 2 hdc in next st] around; join with sl st to first hdc.(40 hdc)

Round 5: Ch 2, [hdc in next 3 sts, 2 hdc in next st] around; join with sl st to first hdc. (50 hdc)

Rounds 6-7: (2 rounds) Ch 2, hdc in each st around; join with sl st to first hdc. (50 hdc)

Round 8: Ch 2, 2 hdc in first st, 2 hdc in each of next 15 sts, hdc in next 34 sts. (66 hdc)

Round 9: Ch 2, [hdc2tog] 16 times. Leave remaining sts unworked. *(image 13)*

Fasten off, leaving a long tail for sewing.

Attaching Hair

1. Position Hair on Head, with puffed up part to the front.

2. Sew the Hair in place, shaping the "puffs" into a wavy pattern. *(image 14 & 15)*

MASK & SNORKEL

Mask

With Color K, ch 40; taking care not to twist ch-sts, sl st in first ch to form a ring.

Round 1: Ch 1, sc in each ch around; join with sl st to first sc. (40 sc)

Rounds 2-3: *(2 rounds)* Ch 1, sc in each st around; join with sl st to first sc. (40 sc)

Change to Color L.

Round 4: Ch 1, working in **back loops** only, sc in each st around; join with sl st to first sc. (40 sc) *(image 16)*

Fasten off. Weave in Color L ends neatly inside Mask.

Cut Color K, leaving a long tail, and weave it back to the beginning of the Mask (to be used for sewing later).

Snorkel

Round 1: With Color M, make a magic ring, 6 sc in ring. (6 sc)

Rounds 2-15: (14 rounds) Sc in each st around. (6 sc)

Fasten off, leaving a long tail for sewing.

Do not stuff.

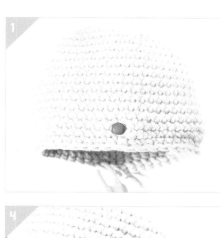

Attaching Snorkel Gear

1. Position and pin Mask on the forehead below the Hair, and sew in place with whipstitches, making sure the stitches are hidden underneath the Mask. *(image 17)*

2. Position Snorkel to side of Mask and sew in place. *(image 18)*

ARM (Make 2)

Round 1: With MC, make a magic ring, 7 sc in ring. (7 sc)

Rounds 2-3: *(2 rounds)* Sc in each st around. (7 sc)

Change to Color H.

Rounds 4-7: *(4 rounds)* Sc in each st around. (7 sc)

Change to Color I.

Round 8: Sc in each st around. (7 sc)

Change to Color H.

Rounds 9-10: *(2 rounds)* Sc in each st around. (7 sc)

Fasten off, leaving a long tail for sewing.

Do not stuff.

LEGS & BODY

Note: *The Legs and Body are worked in one piece.*

First Leg

Round 1: With Color J, make a magic ring, 9 sc in ring. (9 sc)

Round 2: Sc in each st around. (9 sc)

Change to Color H.

Round 3: Working in **back loops** only, sc in each st around. (9 sc)

Rounds 4-7: *(4 rounds)* Sc in each st around. (9 sc)

Change to Color I.

Round 8: Sc in each st around. (9 sc)

Change to Color H.

Round 9: Sc in each st around. (9 sc)

Fasten off.

Stuff leg firmly.

Second Leg

Repeat instructions for First Leg but do not fasten off.

Body

Note: *For Rounds 6 to 12, when changing colors, work over the unused color to carry it around.*

Round 1: *(Joining Legs)* Working on Second Leg, ch 3; working on First Leg, sc in st at inside leg, sc in next 8 sts; working in ch-3, sc in next 3 ch, working on Second Leg, sc in next 9 sts; working in unused loops on other side of ch-3, sc in next 3 ch; working on First Leg, sc in next 6 sts. *(image 19 & 20)*

Mark last st worked as new end of round.

Round 2: [Inc in next st, sc in next 3 sts] 6 times. (30 sc) *(image 21)*

Rounds 3-5: *(3 rounds)* Sc in each st around. (30 sc)

Round 6: Sc in next 21 sts, change to Color I, sc in next 5 sts, change to Color H, sc in next 4 sts. (30 sc)

Round 7: Sc in next 21 sts, change to Color I, sc in next 6 sts, change to Color H, sc in next 3 sts. (30 sc)

Round 8: Sc in next 21 sts, change to Color I, sc in next 7 sts, change to Color H, sc in next 2 sts. (30 sc)

Round 9: Sc in next 21 sts, change to Color I, sc in next 7 sts, change to Color H, sc in next 2 sts. (30 sc)

Round 10: Sc in next 22 sts, change to Color I, sc in next 6 sts, change to Color H, sc in next 2 sts. (30 sc)

Round 11: Sc in next 23 sts, change to Color I, sc in next 5 sts, change to Color H, sc in next 2 sts. (30 sc)

Round 12: Sc in next 24 sts, change to Color I, sc in next 4 sts, change to Color H, sc in next 2 sts. (30 sc)

Round 13: [Sc in next 3 sts, inv-dec] around. (24 sc)

Fasten off, leaving a long tail for sewing.

Stuff Body firmly. *(image 22)*

FLIPPER (Make 2)

Round 1: With Color J, ch 8; starting in 2ⁿᵈ ch from hook, sc in next 6 ch, 3 sc in last ch, working on other side of starting chain, sc in next 6 ch. (15 sc)

Round 2: Sc in each st around. (15 sc)

Round 3: Sc in next st, inv-dec, sc in next 3 sts, inv-dec, sc in next 7 sts. (13 sc)

Round 4: Sc in each st around (13 sc)

Round 5: Sc in next st, inv-dec, sc in next 3 sts, inv-dec, sc in next 5 sts. (11 sc)

Round 6: Sc in each st around. (11 sc)

Round 7: Inv-dec, sc in next 3 sts, inv-dec, sc in next 4 sts. (9 sc) *(image 23)*

Fasten off, leaving a long tail for sewing.

Flipper Detail (using Surface Single Crochet)

Flatten Flipper and make 3 vertical lines on front of Flipper:

Start at right hand side: *Holding Flipper upside down, join Color J with standing sc to Round 7, work 4 more sc in a vertical straight line. (5 sc) Fasten off and weave in ends. *(image 24)*

Repeat from * 2 times more – starting in center, and starting on left-hand side. *(image 25)*

Repeat on other Flipper. *(image 26)*

Attaching Flippers

Sew a Flipper to the bottom of each Leg. *(image 27)*

FINAL DOLL ASSEMBLY

1. Sew Ears to each side of Head, about 6 stitches away from the Eye. *(image 28)*

2. Sew Body to finished Head, adding more stuffing before finishing. *(image 29)*

3. Position Arms and sew in place. *(image 30)*

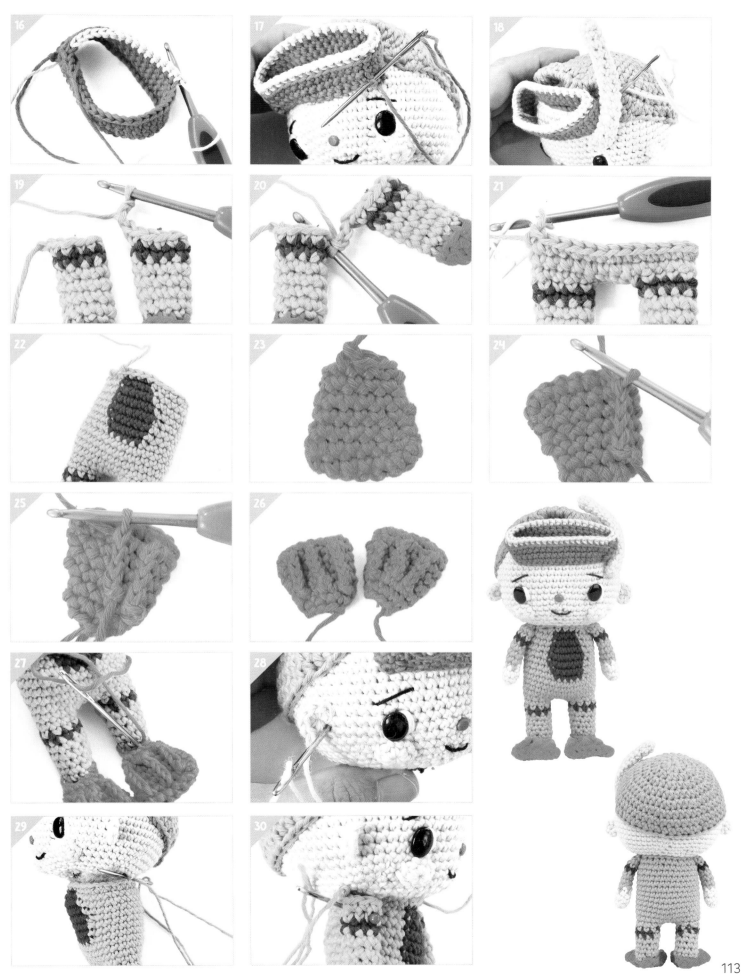

HAIR

Rounds 1-4: Repeat Rounds 1-4 of Josh's Hair.

Rounds 5-6: *(2 rounds)* Ch 2, hdc in each st around; join with sl st to first hdc. (40 hdc)

Work continues in Rows.

Rows 1-5: *(5 rows)* Ch 2, turn, hdc in first st, hdc in next 24 sts. Leave remaining sts unworked. (25 hdc)

Edging & Bangs: Working in sides of rows, sc in first row, 2 sc in each of next 4 rows; working in Round 6, ch 3, sc in 2nd ch from hook, sc in next ch, sl st in first st (on Round 6), sl st in next st, [ch 3, sc in 2nd ch from hook, sc in next ch, sl st in base st, sl st in next st] 3 times (short bangs); [ch 5, sc in 2nd ch from hook, sc in next 3 ch, sl st in base st, sl st in next st] 4 times (medium bangs); [ch 7, sc in 2nd ch from hook, sc in next 5 ch, sl st in base st, sl st in next st] 6 times, ch 7, sc in 2nd ch from hook, sc in next 5 ch, sl st in base st (long bangs); working in sides of rows, 2 sc in each of next 4 rows, sc in last row. *(image 1, 2 & 3)*

Fasten off with Needle Join, leaving a long tail for sewing.

Attaching Hair

1. Position Hair on Head, with bangs to the front, and sew in place. *(image 4)*

ARM (Make 2)

Round 1: With MC, make a magic ring, 7 sc in ring. (7 sc)

Rounds 2-10: *(9 rounds)* Sc in each st around. (7 sc)

Fasten off, leaving a long tail for sewing.

Do not stuff.

LEGS & BODY

***Note**: The Legs and Body are worked in one piece.*

First Leg

Round 1: With Color J, ch 6; starting in 2nd ch from hook, sc in next 4 ch, 3 sc in last ch, working on other side of starting chain, sc in next 4 ch. (11 sc)

Round 2: Inc in the first st, sc in next 4 sts, inc in each of next 2 sts, sc in next 3 sts, inc in last st. (15 sc) *(image 5)*

Change to MC.

Round 3: Working in **back loops** only, sc in each st around. (15 sc) *(image 6)*

Round 4: Sc in next 4 sts, [inv-dec] 4 times, sc in next 3 sts. (11 sc)

Round 5: Sc in next 3 sts, [inv-dec] 2 times, sc in next 4 sts. (9 sc)

Rounds 6-8: *(3 rounds)* Sc in each st around. (9 sc)

Change to Color H.

Round 9: Sc in each st around. (9 sc) *(image 7)*

Fasten off.

Stuff Leg firmly. *(image 8)*

Second Leg

Repeat instructions for First Leg but do not fasten off.

Body

Round 1: *(Joining Legs)* Working on Second Leg, ch 3; working on First Leg, with foot facing forward, sc in st at inside Leg, sc in next next 8 sts; working in ch-3, sc in next 3 ch, working on Second Leg, sc in next next 9 sts; working in unused loops on other side of ch-3, sc in next 3 ch; working on First Leg, sc in next 6 sts. *(image 9)*

Mark last st worked as new end of round.

Round 2: [Inc in next st, sc in next 3 sts] 6 times. (30 sc)

Rounds 3-5: *(3 rounds)* Sc in each st around. (30 sc) *(image 10)*

Change to Color F.

Round 6: Working in **back loops** only, sc in each st around. (30 sc)

Rounds 7-12: *(6 rounds)* Sc in each st around. (30 sc)

Round 13: [Sc in next 3 sts, inv-dec] around. (24 sc) *(image 11)*

Fasten off, leaving a long tail for sewing.

Stuff Body firmly.

Applique

Row 1: With Light Brown Floss and Floss Hook, make a magic ring, 8 sc in ring. (8 sc) *(image 12)*

Change to Dark Brown Floss.

Row 2: Ch 1, turn, sc in each st across. (8 sc) *(image 13 & 14)*

Change to Dark Green Floss.

Row 3: Ch 1, turn, [inc in first st, sc in next st] across. (12 sc) *(image 15)*

Fasten off, leaving a long tail for sewing.

Pants Cuffs

***Note**: Round 1 is worked around Round 9 on each Leg using Surface Single Crochet.*

Round 1: Holding Legs upside down, join Color H with a standing sc to any st on Round 9, sc in next 9 sts; join with sl st to first sc. (10 sc) *(image 16)*

Fasten off and weave in ends.

Repeat on other Leg.

SWIM RING

With Color M, ch 36, taking care not to twist ch-sts, sl st in first ch to form a ring.

Round 1: Ch 1, sc in same ch as joining, sc in next 4 ch, inc in next ch, [sc in next 5 sts, inc in next ch] 5 times; join with sl st to first sc. (42 sc)

Round 2: Ch 1, [sc in next 6 sts, inc in next st] around; join with sl st to first sc. (48 sc)

Round 3: Ch 1, [sc in next 7 sts, inc in next st] around; join with sl st to first sc. (54 sc)

Round 4: Ch 1, [sc in next 8 sts, inc in next st] around; join with sl st to first sc. (60 sc)

Rounds 5-10: *(6 rounds)* Sc in each st around; join with sl st to first sc. (60 sc)

Round 11: [Sc in next 8 sts, inv-dec] around; join with sl st to first sc. (54 sc)

Round 12: [Sc in next 7 sts, inv-dec] around; join with sl st to first sc. (48 sc)

Round 13: [Sc in next 6 sts, inv-dec] around; join with sl st to first sc. (42 sc)

Round 14: [Sc in next 5 sts, inv-dec] around; join with sl st to first sc. (36 sc)

Fasten off, leaving a long end for sewing. *(image 17)*

Swim Ring Assembly

Using long end and yarn needle, whipstitch last round to starting chain, matching stitches, and stuffing as you go. *(image 18 & 19)*

Lion Head

Round 1: With Color M, make a magic ring, 6 sc in ring. (6 sc)

Round 2: Inc in each st around. (12 sc)

Round 3: [Sc in next st, inc in next st] 6 times. (18 sc)

Round 4: [Sc in next 2 sts, inc in next st] 6 times. (24 sc)

Round 5: Working in **back loops** only, sc in each st around. (24 sc)

Round 6: Sc in each st around. (24 sc)

Round 7: Working in **back loops** only, [sc in next 2 sts, inv-dec] 6 times. (18 sc)

Round 8: [Sc in next st, inv-dec] 6 times. (12 sc)

Round 9: [Inv-dec] 6 times. (6 sc)

Fasten off, leaving a long tail for sewing.

Lion Mane

Note: *Round 1 is worked in the unused front loops of Round 4 on Lion Head.*

Round 1: Join Color J with a standing sc to any st of Round 4, sc in next 23 sts; join with sl st to first sc. (24 sc)

Round 2: [3 tr in next st, skip next st, sl st in next st] 8 times. *(image 20)*

Fasten off and weave in ends.

Finishing the Lion Head

Muzzle (Make 2): With Color F, make a magic ring, 5 sc in ring. Fasten off, leaving a long tail for sewing.

Positon Muzzle pieces on face and sew in place.

Nose & Eyes: With Color N and yarn needle, make a French Knot (wrapping yarn 4 times around needle) between the Muzzle pieces for the Nose, then embroider the Eyes.

With Color A, embroider a straight stitch to the left of each Eye for Eye Whites.

Ears (Make 2): With Color M, make a magic ring, 4 sc in ring. Fasten off, leaving a long tail for sewing.

Position and sew on Ears.

Cheeks: With Color B1 and yarn needle, embroider Cheeks. *(image 21)*

Assembling Swim Ring

Sew complete Lion Head to the outer surface of Swim Ring. *(image 22)*

FINAL DOLL ASSEMBLY

1. Sew Ears to each side of Head, about 6 stitches away from the Eye. *(image 23)*

2. Sew Appliqué to center front of Body. *(image 24)*

2. With Color I and yarn needle, embroider straps on the feet (for Sandals). *(image 25)*

3. Sew Body to finished Head, adding more stuffing before finishing. *(image 26)*

4. Position Arms and sew in place. *(image 27)*

5. Place Swim Ring over Doll. *(image 28)*

The Zookeeper

Zara can make even the most timid of animals lively with her gentle presence. Baby elephants hold a special place in her heart, and she enjoys taking them out for a splash in the water.

MATERIALS & TOOLS

HELLO Cotton Yarn

Zara

» **Main Color (MC):** Powder Peach (163) - for Head, Arms & Legs
» **Color A:** White (154) - for Eye Whites & Socks
» **Color B:** Salmon (109) - for Cheeks
» **Color C:** Mint Green (138) - for Hair
» **Color D:** Yellow (123) - for Shoes & Hat, Body, Arms & Badge
» **Color E:** Light Yellow (122) - for Pants & Shirt
» **Color F:** Brown (126) - for Soles of Shoes, Belt and Stripe on Hat

Elephant

» **Color G:** Gray (159) - for Elephant
» **Color H:** Baby Pink (101) - for Elephant Cheeks & Soles

Hook Sizes

» 3mm hook – Main hook
» 3.5mm hook - for Hair
» 5mm hook - for Hat

Other

» Stitch markers
» Yarn needle
» Stuffing
» Craft Glue
» Pins

For Each Doll

» DMC Embroidery Floss - Black
» Embroidery Needle

For Zara

» Safety Eyes - Black Oval 3/8" (10mm) x 2
» Scrapbooking Brad - Orange 5/32" (4mm) x 1 - for Nose
» Mini Buttons x 3 - Brown - for Shirt
» Brown sewing thread & sewing needle

For Elephant

» Safety Eyes - Black Oval 0.2" (5mm) x 2

FINISHED SIZE
Zara - About 7¼" (18.5cm) tall
Elephant - About 4½" (11.5cm) tall

SKILL LEVEL
Intermediate

PATTERN NOTES

The Main hook is used throughout, unless otherwise stated.

SPECIAL STITCHES

Bobble (bob) (refer to Special Crochet Stitches): Yarn over, insert hook in stitch or space specified and pull up a loop (3 loops on hook), yarn over and draw through 2 loops on hook (2 loops remain); *yarn over and insert hook in same stitch or space and pull up a loop, yarn over and draw through two loops on hook; repeat from * 3 times more (6 loops on hook), yarn over and draw through all 6 loops; ch 1 to secure.
Note: *The ch-1 does not count as a stitch and is skipped when working the next round.*

Surface Single Crochet (refer to Tips & Techniques): With right side of crochet piece facing, work between the stitches. Start with a slip knot on the hook and insert it in specified stitch and out in next stitch; pull up a loop (2 loops on hook); yarn over hook and draw through both loops on hook. (standing surface single crochet made)
For following stitches, insert hook in stitch where the hook came out of and out again in next stitch; pull up a loop (2 loops on hook); yarn over and draw through both loops. (Surface single crochet made)

ZARA

HEAD

Round 1: With MC, make a magic ring, 6 sc in ring. (6 sc)

Round 2: Inc in each st around. (12 sc)

Round 3: [Sc in next st, inc in next st] 6 times. (18 sc)

Round 4: [Sc in next 2 sts, inc in next st] 6 times. (24 sc)

Round 5: [Sc in next 3 sts, inc in next st] 6 times. (30 sc)

Round 6: [Sc in next 4 sts, inc in next st] 6 times. (36 sc)

Round 7: [Sc in next 5 sts, inc in next st] 6 times. (42 sc)

Round 8: [Sc in next 6 sts, inc in next st] 6 times. (48 sc)

Round 9: [Sc in next 7 sts, inc in next st] 6 times. (54 sc)

Round 10: [Sc in next 8 sts, inc in next st] 6 times. (60 sc)

Rounds 11-21: *(11 rounds)* Sc in each st around. (60 sc)

Round 22: [Sc in next 8 sts, inv-dec] 6 times. (54 sc) *(image 1)*

Round 23: [Sc in next 7 sts, inv-dec] 6 times. (48 sc)

Round 24: [Sc in next 6 sts, inv-dec] 6 times. (42 sc)

Add Facial Features:

1. Nose - position brad at front of Head (about 27th stitch on Round 20) and lock in place. *(image 2 & 3)*

2. Eyes - position on Round 19, about 6 stitches from either side of Nose and secure in place. *(image 4 & 5)*

3. Eye Whites - using Color A and yarn needle, make 3-4 vertical straight stitches (the same height as Eyes) to the left of each Eye. Knot and secure the yarn on the inside of the Head. *(image 6)*

Continue crocheting:

Round 25: [Sc in next 5 sts, inv-dec] 6 times. (36 sc)

Round 26: [Sc in next 4 sts, inv-dec] 6 times. (30 sc)

Round 27: [Sc in next 3 sts, inv-dec] 6 times. (24 sc)

Start stuffing Head, adding more as you go.

Round 28: [Sc in next 2 sts, inv-dec] 6 times. (18 sc)

Round 29: [Sc in next st, inv-dec] 6 times. (12 sc)

Round 30: [Inv dec] 6 times. (6 sc) Fasten off.

Close the opening securely and leave a long tail (for Eye Indentations). *(image 7)*

Cheek (Make 2)

Round 1: With Color B, make a magic ring, 6 sc in ring. (6 sc)

Fasten off with Needle Join, leaving a long tail for sewing.

FINISHING THE FACE

Eye Indentations

Using long tail on Head and yarn needle:

1. Bring needle up from base of Head and out next to the nose-side of Eye. *(image 8)*

2. Insert needle in next stitch, bringing it out at base of Head. Gently tug yarn to create a slight indentation at the Eye. *(image 9)*

3. Repeat steps 1 & 2 for other Eye. *(image 10 & 11)*

4. Secure yarn tail with a knot at base of Head and trim excess yarn.

Cheeks - Position the Cheeks below each Eye and sew in place, bringing the yarn out at base of Head. Secure with a knot and trim excess yarn. *(image 12)*

Eyebrows & Mouth

Using Black Embroidery Floss and needle:

1. Bring needle up from base of Head and embroider Eyebrows above each Eye – by making a diagonal straight stitch from Round 16 to Round 17, about 4 stitches long. *(image 13)*

2. After Eyebrows, bring needle down through Head to create a Mouth on Round 22, centered under the Nose – by making a loose horizontal straight stitch, about 3 stitches long, bringing needle out at base of Head. Tie ends in a knot to secure and trim excess yarn. *(image 14)*

3. Optional: Apply glue on Mouth, and use pins to shape the smile while the glue dries. *(image 15 & 16)*

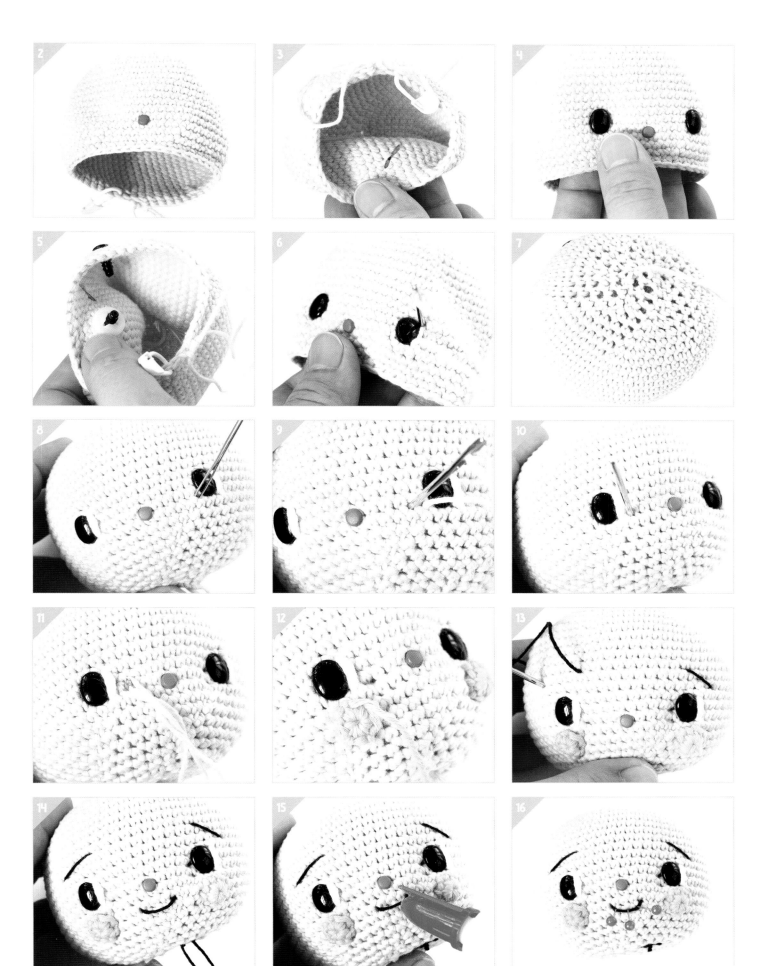

HAIR

Rounds 1-10: With Color C and Hair hook, repeat Rounds 1-10 of the Head.

Rounds 11-13: *(3 rounds)* Ch 1, hdc in each st around; join with sl st to first hdc. (60 hdc)

Work continues in Rows

Row 14: *(First Bangs)* Ch 1, sc in next 2 sts, [bob in next st, sc in next st] 5 times. Leave remaining sts unworked. (5 bobble sts & 7 sc) *(image 17)*

Row 15: Ch 1, turn, sc in each st across. (12 sc) *(image 18)*

Row 16: Ch 1, turn, [inv-dec, bob in next st, sc in next st] 3 times; working in sides of rows, sc in each of next 2 rows, working in Round 13, sl st in next st. (3 bobble sts & 8 sc) *(image 19)*

Row 17: *(Second Bangs)* [Sc in next st, bob in next st] 5 times, sc in next 2 sts. (5 bobble sts & 7 sc) *(image 20)*

Row 18: Ch 1, turn, sc in each st across. (12 sc)

Row 19: Ch 1, turn, [sc in next st, bob in next st, inv-dec] 3 times; working in sides of rows, sc in each of next 2 rows. (3 bobble sts & 8 sc)

Row 20: Working in Round 13, sl st in next st, [inv-dec, sc in next st] 11 times, sc in last st. (23 sc). *(image 21)*

Fasten off, leaving a long tail for sewing.

Pigtails (Make 2)

First Pigtail: With Color C and Hair hook, ch 20, hdc in 2nd ch from hook, hdc in next 17 ch, (hdc, sl st) in last ch. (19 hdc & 1 sl st)

Next Pigtail: *Ch 20, hdc in 2nd ch from hook, hdc in next 18 ch, sl st in same last ch on First Pigtail; repeat from * once more. (3 pigtails) *(image 22)*

Fasten off, leaving a long tail for sewing.

Attaching Hair

1. Position Hair on Head, with Bangs facing forward, and sew into place. *(image 23)*

2. Position Pigtails on either side at edge of Bangs, and sew only the top part of Pigtails to Head, leaving the locks flowing. *(image 24)*

3. Braid the Pigtails and using a strand of Color D, tie the braid to secure. *(image 25)*

LEGS & BODY

Note: *For this pattern, the Body will be worked from the Legs up in one piece.*

First Leg

Round 1: With Color F, ch 8; starting in 2nd ch from hook, sc in next 6 ch, 3 sc in last ch, working on other side of starting chain, sc in next 6 ch. (15 sc)

Round 2: Inc in first st, sc in next 6 sts, inc in next 2 sts, sc in next 5 sts, inc in last st. (19 sc)

Change to Color D.

Round 3: Working in **back loops** only, sc in each st around. (19 sc)

Round 4: Sc in each st around. (19 sc)

Round 5: Sc in next 8 sts, [inv-dec] 3 times, sc in next 5 sts. (16 sc)

Round 6: Sc in next 7 sts, [inv-dec] 4 times, sc in last st. (12 sc)

Change to Color A.

Round 7: Working in **back loops** only, sc in each st around. (12 sc)

Rounds 8-9: *(2 rounds)* Sc in each st around. (12 sc)

Change to MC.

Rounds 10-11: *(2 rounds)* Sc in each st around. (12 sc)

Change to Color E.

Round 12: Inc in each st around. (24 sc)

Round 13: Sc in each st around. (24 sc) *(image 26)*

Fasten off.

Stuff Leg firmly.

Second Leg

Repeat instructions for First Leg but do not fasten off.

Body

Joining Round: Working on Second Leg, ch 2; working on First Leg, with foot facing forward, sc in st at inside Leg, sc in next 23 sts; working in ch-2, sc in next 2 ch; working on Second Leg, sc in next 24 sts; working in unused loops on other side of ch-2, sc in next 2 ch; working on First Leg, sc in next 11 sts. *(image 27 & 28)*

Mark last st worked as new end of round.

Round 2: [Inv-dec] 14 times, sc in next st, [inv-dec] 5 times, sc in next st, [inv-dec] 6 times. (27 sc)

Round 3: [Sc in next 2 sts, inc in next st] 9 times. (36 sc)

Round 4: Sc in each st around. (36 sc)

Round 5: [Sc in next 4 sts, inv-dec] 6 times. (30 sc)

Rounds 6-16: (11 rounds) Sc in each st around (30 sc)

Round 17: [Sc in next 3 sts, inv-dec] 6 times. (24 sc)

Fasten off, leaving a long tail for sewing. *(image 29)*

Stuff body firmly.

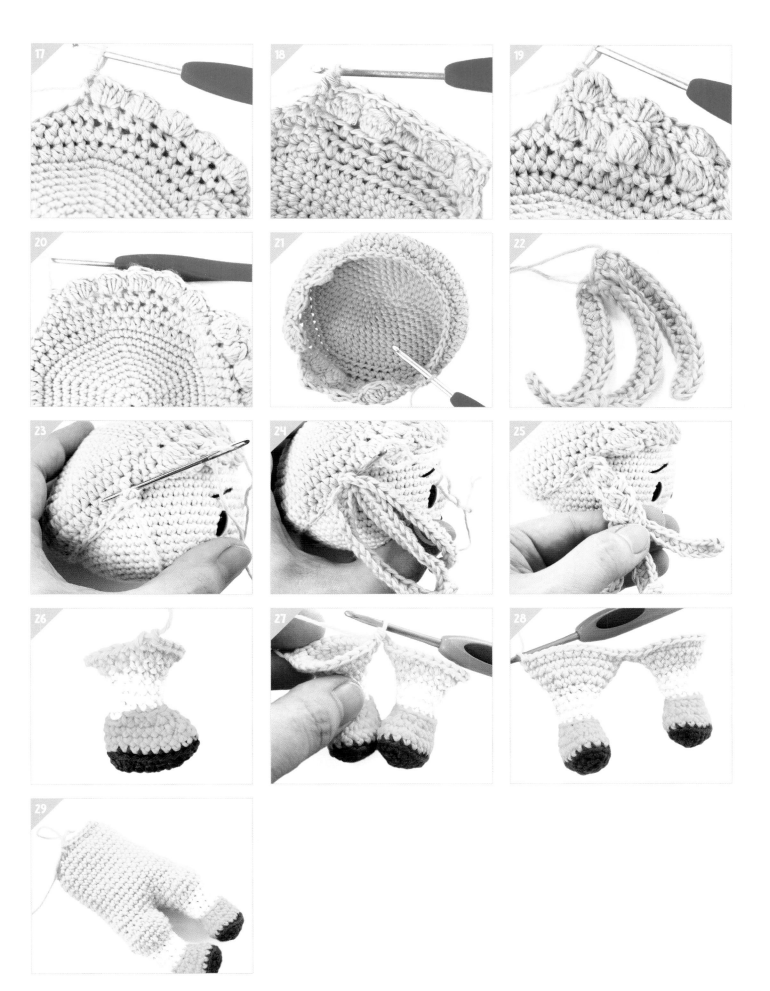

Shirt Detail

Note: *Use Surface Single Crochet in a straight line from Round 17 through Round 25.*

Holding Body with front facing up and Legs pointing away, join Color E with a standing sc in st at center front on Round 17, sc in each of next 8 rounds. (9 sc) *(image 30)*

Fasten off and weave in ends.

Adding Buttons

Using sewing thread and needle, sew the 3 mini buttons next to the Shirt Detail line. Knot the thread ends inside the Body. *(image 31)*

Pants Cuffs

Note: *Round 1 is worked around Round 13 on each Leg using Surface Single Crochet.*

Round 1: Holding Legs upside down, join Color E with standing sc to st at center back on Round 13, sc in next 12 sts; join with sl st to first sc. (13 sc)

Round 2: Ch 1, Inc in each st around; join with sl st to first sc. (26 sc)

Fasten off and weave in ends. *(image 32)*

Repeat on other Leg.

Collar

Row 1: With Color E, ch 32, starting in 2nd ch from hook, dec (using next 2 ch), sc in next 27 sts, dec (using last 2 ch). (29 sc)

Row 2: Ch 1, turn, working in **back loops** only, sc in each st across. (29 sc)

Fasten off, leaving a long tail for sewing.

ARM (Make 2)

Round 1: With MC, make a magic ring, 6 sc in ring. (6 sc)

Round 2: Inc in each st around. (12 sc)

Rounds 3-4: *(2 rounds)* Sc in each st around. (12 sc)

Round 5: [Inv-dec] 3 times, sc in the next 6 sts. (9 sc)

Rounds 6-12: (7 rounds) Sc in each st around. (9 sc)

Change to Color E.

Round 13: Sc in each st around. (9 sc)

Fasten off, leaving a long tail for sewing.

Stuff Arm lightly.

Sleeves

Note: *Round 1 is worked around Round 13 on each Arm using Surface Single Crochet.*

Round 1: Holding Arm upside down, join Color E with standing sc to any st on Round 13, sc in next 9 sts, sl st to first st. (10 sc)

Round 2: Ch 1 [Sc in next st, inc in next st] 5 times sl st to first st. (15 sc) *(image 33)*

Round 3: Ch 1 Sc in each st around sl st to first st. (15 sc)

Fasten off and weave in ends.

Repeat on other Arm. *(image 34)*

BELT

Row 1: With Color F, ch 3, starting in 2nd ch from hook, hdc in each st across. (2 hdc)

Rows 2-22: *(21 rows)* Ch 1, turn. Hdc in each st across (2 hdc)

Fasten off, leaving a long tail for sewing.

Belt Buckle

Row 1: With Color F, ch 4, starting in 2nd ch from hook, sc in each st across. (3 sc)

Rows 2-4: *(3 rows)* Ch 1, turn, Sc in each st across (3 sc)

Fasten off, leaving a long tail for sewing.

HAT

Hint: *Use 2 separate balls of yarn – holding one strand from each.*

Rounds 1-8: With double strand of Color D and Hat hook, repeat Rounds 1-8 of Head.

Rounds 9-10: *(2 rounds)* Sc in each st around. (48 sc)

Change to Color F.

Rounds 11-12: *(2 rounds)* Sc in each st around. (48 sc)

Change to Color D.

Round 13: Working in **back loops** only, [sc in next 7 sts, inc in next st] around. (54 sc)

Round 14: [Sc in next st, inc in next st] around. (81 sc) *(image 35 & 36)*

Fasten off and weave in ends.

FINAL DOLL ASSEMBLY

1. Sew Body to finished Head, adding more stuffing before finishing. *(image 37)*

2. Wrap Collar around neck, with opening at front, and sew in place. *(image 38)*

3. Position the Arms and sew in place. *(image 39)*

4. Wrap Belt around Body, with join at back, and sew in place. *(image 40)*

5. With Color D and yarn needle, embroider a square border on the Buckle using backstitches.

6. Sew Buckle to Belt at center front. *(image 41)*

7. With Color F and yarn needle, embroider 2 "X"s on each shoe (for shoelaces). *(image 42)*

8. Place Hat on Doll's Head. *(image 43)*

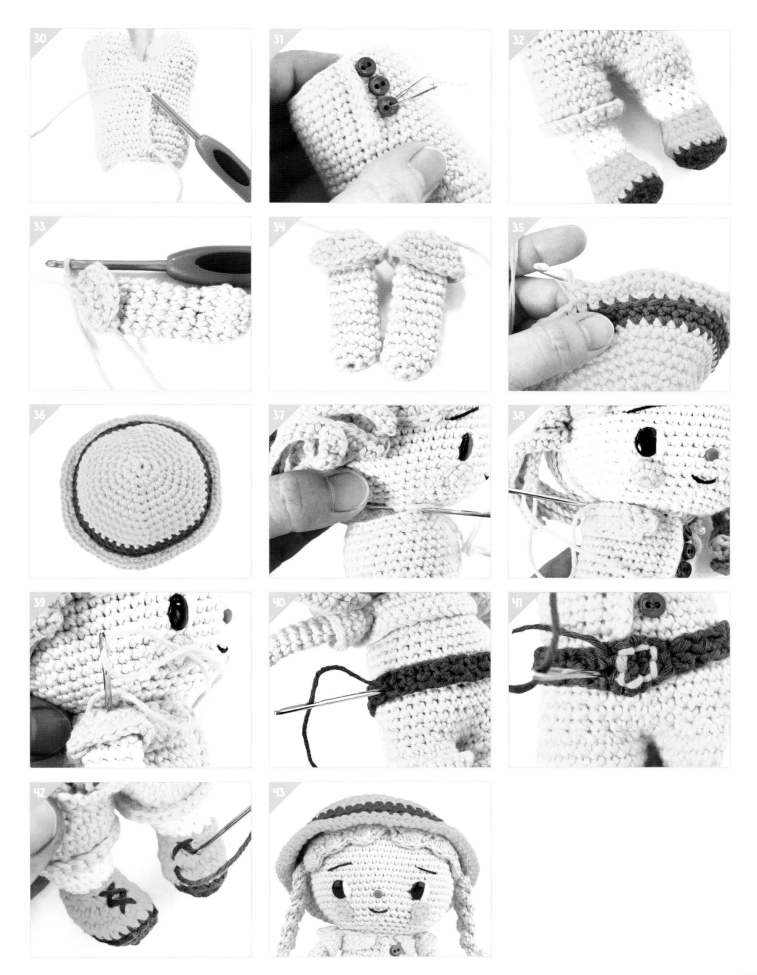

ELEPHANT

HEAD

Rounds 1-9: With Color G, repeat Rounds 1-9 of Doll's Head.

Rounds 10–15: (6 rounds) Sc in each st around. (54 sc)

Round 16: Sc in next 20 sts, inc in each of next 3 sts, sc in next 8 sts, inc in each of next 3 sts, sc in next 20 sts. (60 sc)

Round 17: Sc in next 21 sts, inc in each of next 3 sts, sc in next 11 sts, inc in each of next 3 sts, sc in next 22 sts. (66 sc)

Round 18: Sc in next 21 sts, [inv-dec] 3 times, sc in next 11 sts, [inv-dec] 3 times, sc in next 22 sts. (60 sc)

Round 19: Sc in next 20 sts, [inv-dec] 3 times, sc in next 8 sts, [inv-dec] 3 times, sc in next 20 sts. (54 sc)

Round 20: [Sc in next 7 sts, inv-dec] 6 times. (48 sc)

Round 21: [Sc in next 6 sts, inv-dec] 6 times. (42 sc)

Insert Safety Eyes

- Position Eyes on Round 16 at center front of Head, with 9 sts between them, and secure with locking washer.

Round 22: [Sc in next 5 sts, inv-dec] 6 times. (36 sc)

Round 23: [Sc in next 4 sts, inv-dec] 6 times. (30 sc)

Round 24: [Sc in next 3 sts, inv-dec] 6 times. (24 sc)

Round 25: [Sc in next 2 sts, inv-dec] 6 times. (18 sc)

Start stuffing Head, adding more as you go.

Round 26: [Sc in next st, inv-dec] 6 times. (12 sc)

Round 27: [Inv dec] 6 times. (6 sc)

Fasten off and close the opening securely, leaving a long tail (to make the Eye Indentations).

Cheek (Make 2)

Round 1: With Color H, make a magic ring, 6 sc in ring. (6 sc)

Fasten off with Needle Join, leaving a long tail for sewing.

TRUNK

Round 1: With Color G, make a magic ring, 8 sc in ring. (8 sc)

Rounds 2-7: *(6 rounds)* Sc in each st around. (8 sc)

Round 8: [Sc in next st, inc in next st] 3 times, sc in next 2 sts. (11 sc)

Round 9: [Sc in next 2 sts, inc in next st] 3 times, sc in next 2 sts. (14 sc)

Fasten off, leaving a long tail for sewing.

Flatten piece. (Trunk is not stuffed.)

EAR (Make 2)

Rounds 1-7: With Color G, repeat Rounds 1-7 of Doll's Head.

Fasten off, leaving a long tail for sewing.

BODY

Rounds 1-6: With Color G, repeat Rounds 1-6 of Doll's Head.

Rounds 7-14: (8 rounds) Sc in each st around. (36 sc)

Round 15: [Sc in next 4 sts, inv-dec] 6 times. (30 sc)

Round 16: [Sc in next 3 sts, inv-dec] 6 times. (24 sc)

Fasten off, leaving a long tail for sewing. Stuff firmly.

LEGS

Front Leg (Make 2)

Round 1: With Color H, make a magic ring, 6 sc in ring. (6 sc)

Round 2: Inc in each st around. (12 sc)

Change to Color G.

Round 3: [Sc in next st, inc in next st] 6 times. (18 sc)

Round 4: Working in **back loops** only, sc in each st around. (18 sc)

Round 5: Sc in next 6 sts, [inv-dec] 3 times, sc in next 6 sts. (15 sc)

Round 6: Sc in next 4 sts, [inv-dec] 3 times, sc in next 5 sts. (12 sc)

Rounds 7-11: *(5 rounds)* Sc in each st around. (12 sc)

Fasten off, leaving a long tail for sewing.

Stuff firmly.

Hind Leg (Make 2)

Rounds 1-6: Repeat Rounds 1-6 of the Front Leg.

Rounds 7-9: (3 rounds) Sc in each st around. (12 sc)

Fasten off, leaving a long tail for sewing.

Stuff firmly.

TAIL

Round 1: With Color G, make a magic ring, 6 sc in ring. (6 sc)

Rounds 2-11: (10 rounds) Sc in each st around. (6 sc)

Fasten off, leaving a long tail for sewing.

FINAL ELEPHANT ASSEMBLY

1. Make Eye Indentations, following Doll's instructions. *(image 44 & 45)*

2. Position Cheeks below each Eye and sew in place. Knot the yarn ends at base of Head.

3. Using black embroidery floss, embroider the Eyebrows (above each Eye on Round 12) with a straight stitch, 2 stitches long.

4. Position and sew the Trunk between Eyes and Cheeks, in a slightly slanted manner. (The thicker part of the trunk should be at the top.) *(image 46)*

5. Bend the Ears in a "C"- shape and sew to either side of Head. *(image 47)*

6. Sew Body onto Head. *(image 48)*

7. Sew on Front Legs and Hind Legs. *(image 49 & 50)*

8. Sew on Tail. *(image 51)*

Little
Scottie

No adventure is too big for Little Scottie, who dreams of sailing the seven seas. He loves to travel the world on his little boat and make new friends.

MATERIALS & TOOLS

HELLO Cotton Yarn

» **Main Color (MC):** Powder Peach (163) - for Head, Ears & Arms
» **Color A:** White (154) - for Eye Whites, Collar & Hat
» **Color B:** Baby Pink (101) - for Cheeks
» **Color C:** Turquoise (134) - for Hair
» **Color D:** Sky Blue (147) - for Pants, Shirt & Sleeves
» **Color E:** Dusty Blue (145) - for Shoes
» **Color F:** Bright Orange (118) - for Shoes & Collar Details

Hook Sizes

» 3mm hook
» 3.5mm hook – for Hair

Other

» Stitch markers
» Yarn needle
» Stuffing
» Craft Glue
» Pins
» Safety Eyes - Black Oval 3/8" (10mm) x 2
» Scrapbooking Brad - Orange 5/32" (4mm) x 1 - for Nose
» DMC Embroidery Floss - Black
» Embroidery Needle

FINISHED SIZE
About 7" (18cm) tall

SKILL LEVEL
Intermediate

PATTERN NOTES

The smaller size hook is used throughout, unless otherwise stated.

When working double crochet rows or rounds, the first ch-2 does not count as the first stitch. The first dc of a row is worked in the last stitch made on the previous row. The first dc of a round is worked in the same stitch as the previous round's join.

SPECIAL STITCHES

Surface Single Crochet (refer to Tips & Techniques): With right side of crochet piece facing, work between the stitches. Start with a slip knot on the hook and insert it in specified stitch and out in next stitch; pull up a loop (2 loops on hook); yarn over hook and draw through both loops on hook. (standing surface single crochet made)
For following stitches, insert hook in stitch where the hook came out of and out again in next stitch; pull up a loop (2 loops on hook); yarn over and draw through both loops. (Surface single crochet made)

SCOTTIE

HEAD

Round 1: With MC, make a magic ring, 6 sc in ring. (6 sc)

Round 2: Inc in each st around. (12 sc)

Round 3: [Sc in next st, inc in next st] 6 times. (18 sc)

Round 4: [Sc in next 2 sts, inc in next st] 6 times. (24 sc)

Round 5: [Sc in next 3 sts, inc in next st] 6 times. (30 sc)

Round 6: [Sc in next 4 sts, inc in next st] 6 times. (36 sc)

Round 7: [Sc in next 5 sts, inc in next st] 6 times. (42 sc)

Round 8: [Sc in next 6 sts, inc in next st] 6 times. (48 sc)

Round 9: [Sc in next 7 sts, inc in next st] 6 times. (54 sc)

Round 10: [Sc in next 8 sts, inc in next st] 6 times. (60 sc)

Rounds 11-21: *(11 rounds)* Sc in each st around. (60 sc)

Round 22: [Sc in next 8 sts, inv-dec] 6 times. (54 sc) *(image 1)*

Round 23: [Sc in next 7 sts, inv-dec] 6 times. (48 sc)

Round 24: [Sc in next 6 sts, inv-dec] 6 times. (42 sc)

Add Facial Features:

1. Nose - position brad at front of Head (about 27th stitch on Round 20) and lock in place. *(image 2 & 3)*

2. Eyes - position on Round 19, about 6 stitches from either side of Nose and secure in place. *(image 4 & 5)*

3. Eye Whites - using Color A and yarn needle, make 3-4 vertical straight stitches (the same height as Eyes) to the left of each Eye. Knot and secure the yarn on the inside of the Head. *(image 6)*

Continue crocheting:

Round 25: [Sc in next 5 sts, inv-dec] 6 times. (36 sc)

Round 26: [Sc in next 4 sts, inv-dec] 6 times. (30 sc)

Round 27: [Sc in next 3 sts, inv-dec] 6 times. (24 sc)

Start stuffing Head, adding more as you go.

Round 28: [Sc in next 2 sts, inv-dec] 6 times. (18 sc)

Round 29: [Sc in next st, inv-dec] 6 times. (12 sc)

Round 30: [Inv dec] 6 times. (6 sc) Fasten off.

Close the opening securely and leave a long tail (for Eye Indentations). *(image 7)*

Cheek (Make 2)

Round 1: With Color B, make a magic ring, 6 sc in ring. (6 sc)

Fasten off with Needle Join, leaving a long tail for sewing.

FINISHING THE FACE

Eye Indentations

Using long tail on Head and yarn needle:

1. Bring needle up from base of Head and out next to the nose-side of Eye. *(image 8)*

2. Insert needle in next stitch, bringing it out at base of Head. Gently tug yarn to create a slight indentation at the Eye. *(image 9)*

3. Repeat steps 1 & 2 for other Eye. *(image 10 & 11)*

4. Secure yarn tail with a knot at base of Head and trim excess yarn.

Cheeks - Position the Cheeks below each Eye and sew in place, bringing the yarn out at base of Head. Secure with a knot and trim excess yarn. *(image 12)*

Eyebrows & Mouth

Using Black Embroidery Floss and needle:

1. Bring needle up from base of Head and embroider Eyebrows above each Eye – by making a diagonal straight stitch from Round 16 to Round 17, about 4 stitches long. *(image 13)*

2. After Eyebrows, bring needle down through Head to create a Mouth on Round 22, centered under the Nose – by making a loose horizontal straight stitch, about 4 stitches long, bringing needle out at base of Head. Tie ends in a knot to secure and trim excess yarn. *(image 14)*

3. Optional: Apply glue on Mouth, and use pins to shape the smile while the glue dries. *(image 15 & 16)*

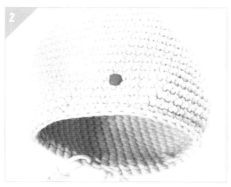

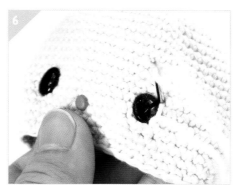
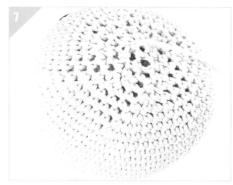
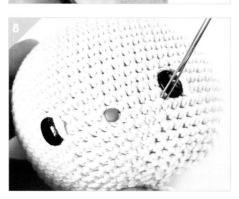
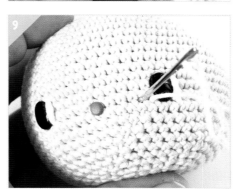
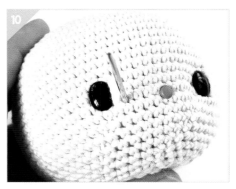

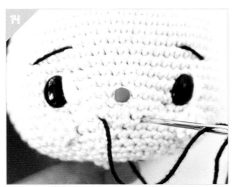

HAIR

Rounds 1-10: With Color C and larger hook, repeat Rounds 1-10 of the Head.

Rounds 11-13: *(3 rounds)* Sc in each st around. (60 sc) Work continues in Rows.

Row 1: Ch 1, turn, sc in each of the next 38 sts. (38 sc) Leave remaining sts unworked.

Rows 2-8: *(7 rows)* Ch 1, turn, sc in each st across. (38 sc)

Edging & Bangs: Working in sides of rows, sc in each of next 7 rows; ch 3, sc in 2nd ch from hook, sc in last ch, sl st in same st as sc on last row; working in Round 13, sl st in next st, [ch 3, sc in 2nd ch from hook, sc in last ch, sl st in same st as last sl st made, sl st in next st] 9 times, [ch 6, sc in 2nd ch from hook, sc in next 4 ch, sl st in same st as last sl st made, sl st in next st] 12 times; working in sides of rows, sc in each of next 7 rows. (14 sc, 10 short bangs & 12 long bangs) *(image 17 & 18)*

Fasten off with Needle Join, leaving a long tail for sewing.

EAR (Make 2)

Round 1: With MC, make a magic ring, 6 sc in ring. (6 sc)

Fasten off, leaving a long tail for sewing.

LEGS & BODY

Note: *The Legs and Body are worked in one piece.*

First Leg

Round 1: With Color E, ch 6; starting in 2nd ch from hook, sc in next 4 ch, 3 sc in last ch, working on other side of starting chain, sc in next 4 ch. (11 sc)

Round 2: Inc in first st, sc in next 4 sts, inc in each of next 2 sts, sc in next 3 sts, inc in last st. (15 sc)

Round 3: Working in **back loops** only, sc in each st around. (15 sc)

Round 4: Sc in next 4sts, [inv-dec] 4 times, sc in next 3 sts. (11 sc)

Change to Color D.

Round 5: Sc in next 3 sts, [inv-dec] 2 times, sc in next 4 sts. (9 sc)

Round 6: [Sc in next 2 sts, inc in next st] around. (12 sc).

Round 7: [Sc in next 3 sts, inc in next st] around. (15 sc).

Rounds 8-10: *(3 rounds)* Sc in each st around. (15 sc)

Fasten off. *(image 19)* Stuff leg firmly.

Second Leg

Repeat instructions for First Leg but do not fasten off.

Body

Joining Round: Working on Second Leg, ch 3; working on First Leg, with foot facing forward, sc in st at inside Leg, sc in next 14 sts; working in ch-3, sc in next 3 ch; working on Second Leg, sc in next 15 sts; working in unused loops on other side of ch-3, sc in next 3 ch; working on First Leg, sc in next 7 sts. *(image 20 & 21)*

Mark last st worked as new end of round.

Round 2: [Sc in next 4 sts, inv-dec] around. (30 sc)

Rounds 3-6: *(4 rounds)* Sc in each st around. (30 sc) Change to MC.

Rounds 7-12: *(6 rounds)* Sc in each st around. (30 sc)

Round 13: [Sc in next 3 sts, inv-dec] around. (24 sc)

Fasten off, leaving a long tail for sewing. *(image 22)*

Stuff body firmly.

Pants Cuffs

Note: *Round 1 is worked around Round 5 on each Leg using Surface Single Crochet.*

Round 1: Holding Legs upside down, join Color D with standing sc on any st of Round 5, sc in next 9 sts; join with sl st to first sc. (10 sc) *(image 23)*

Fasten off and weave in ends.

Repeat on other Leg.

Shirt

Note: *Round 1 is worked around Round 13 on Body using Surface Single Crochet.*

Round 1: Holding Body upside down, join Color D with standing sc to center back st on Round 13, sc in next 24 sts; join with sl st to first sc. (25 sc) *(image 24 & 25)*

Round 2: Ch 1, [sc in next 3 sts, inc in next st] 6 times, sc in last st; join with sl st to first sc. (31 sc)

Round 3: Ch 1, [sc in next 4 sts, inc in next st] 6 times, sc in last st; join with sl st to first sc. (37 sc)

Round 4: Ch 1, sc in next 11 sts, inc in next st, sc in next 12 sts, inc in next st, sc in next 11 sts, inc in next st; join with sl st to first sc. (40 sc) *(image 26)*

Round 5: Ch 1, sc in next 12 sts, inc in next st, sc in next 13 sts, inc in next st, sc in next 12 sts, inc in next st; join with sl st to first sc. (43 sc)

Rounds 6-13: *(8 rounds)* Ch 1, sc in each st around; join with sl st to first sc. (43 sc)

Round 14: Sl st in each st around. (43 sl st) *(image 27)*

Fasten off with Needle Join and weave in ends.

COLLAR

Row 1: With Color A, ch 18, starting in 2nd ch from hook, dc in each st across. (17 dc)

Rows 2-3: *(2 rows)* Ch 2, turn, dc in each st across. (17 dc)

Last Row: *(Ties & Edging)* *Ch 15, working in 2nd ch from hook, dc in each ch across*; sl st in last dc on Row 3 (First Tie made); working in Row 3, sc in next 16 sts; repeat from * to * once, sl st in base of last dc (Second Tie made); evenly sc around edges of Collar, ending at base of First Tie. *(image 28)*

Fasten off and weave in ends.

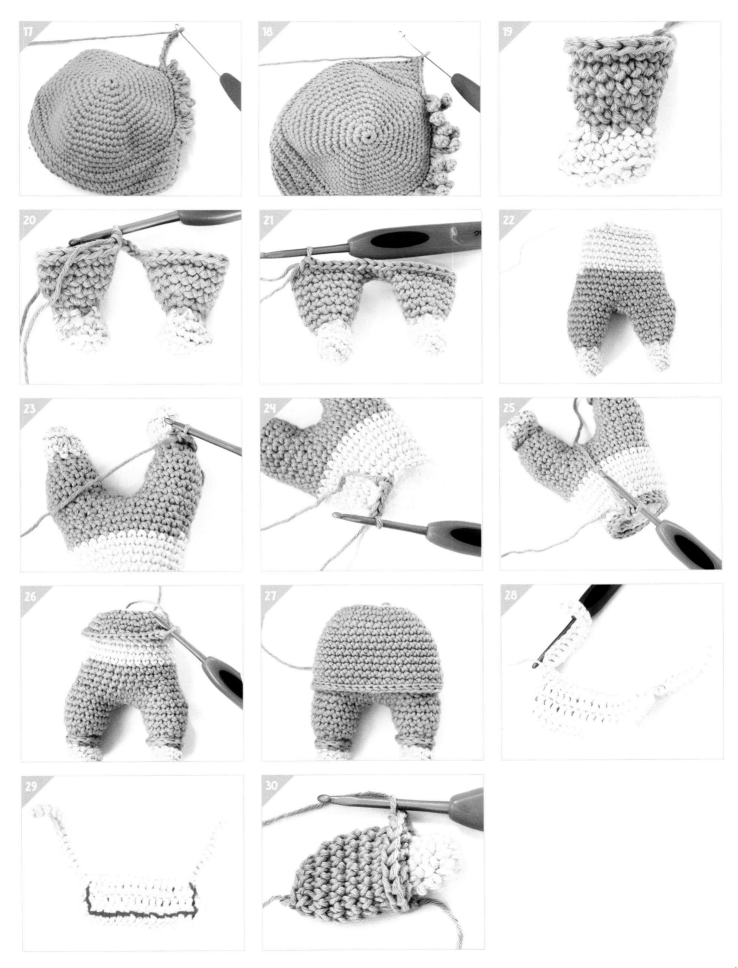

Collar Detail

With Color F and yarn needle, embroider a border using small backstitches around three sides of Collar. *(image 29)*

ARM (Make 2)

Round 1: With MC, make a magic ring, 7 sc in ring. (7 sc)

Rounds 2-4: *(3 rounds)* Sc in each st around. (7 sc)

Change to Color D.

Round 5: Inc in each st around. (14 sc)

Rounds 6-10: *(5 rounds)* Sc in each st around. (14 sc)

Round 11: [Inv-dec] 7 times. (7 sc)

Fasten off, leaving a long tail for sewing.

Stuff Arm lightly.

Sleeve Cuffs

Note: *Round 1 is worked around Round 6 on each Arm using Surface Single Crochet.*

Round 1: Holding Arm upside down, join Color D with standing sc to any st on Round 6, sc in next 14 sts; join with sl st to first sc. (15 sc) *(image 30)*

Fasten off with Needle Join and weave in ends.

Repeat on other Arm.

HAT

Round 1: With Color A, make a magic ring, 6 sc in ring. (6sc)

Round 2: Inc in each st around. (12 sc)

Round 3: [Sc in next st, inc in next st] 6 times. (18 sc)

Round 4: [Sc in next 2 sts, inc in next st] 6 times. (24 sc)

Rounds 5-7: *(3 rounds)* Sc in each st around. (24 sc)

Round 8: Working in **back loops** only, [sc in next 3 sts, inc in next st] 6 times. (30 sc)

Round 9: [Sc in next 4 sts, inc in next st] 6 times. (36 sc)

Round 10: Sc in each st around. (36 sc)

Fasten off, leaving a long end for sewing.

Fold up the brim. *(image 31)*

Hat Detail

Using Color D and yarn needle, embroider small backstitches around Round 9 of Hat Brim. *(image 32)*

FINAL DOLL ASSEMBLY

1. Position Hair on Head and sew in place. *(image 33)*

2. Sew Ears to the sides of Head, about 4 stitches away from each Eye. *(image 34)*

3. Sew Body to finished Head, adding more stuffing before finishing. *(image 35)*

4. With Color F and yarn needle, embroider small backstitches around base of each Shoe. *(image 36)*

5. With Color A, embroider 2 rows of small backstitches around each Leg. *(image 37)*

6. Position the Arms and sew in place. Repeat the 2 rows of backstitches on each Arm. *(image 38 & 39)*

7. Place Collar around neck, with the Ties in front. Using Color F and yarn needle, sew the crossed Ties to the Body using several stitches, bringing the yarn back down into the Body to the secure. *(image 40, 41 & 42)*

8. Position Hat on Head – slightly off-center. Sew in place, stuffing lightly as you go, making sure the seams are hidden underneath the brim. *(image 43, 44 & 45)*

samantha
The Big Sister

When mommy and daddy are busy, Sammy knows she's got to take charge. Helping with the chores, feeding the baby, cleaning up after herself - this big sister is the best little helper you can have when there's a tiny newborn at home.

MATERIALS & TOOLS

HELLO Cotton Yarn

» **Main Color (MC):** Powder Peach (163) - for Head, Body, Arms & Legs
» **Color A:** White (154) - for Eye Whites
» **Color B:** Salmon (109) - for Cheeks
» **Color C:** Orchid (141) - for Hair & Ponytail
» **Color D:** Lavender (140) - for Dress & Body
» **Color E:** Cream (156) - for Body, Dress Edging & Baby Carrier
» **Color F:** Dusty Blue (145) - for Baby Body, Arms & Legs
» **Color G:** Black (160) - for Shoes
» **Color H:** Dark Pink (104) - for Cherry Hair Tie
» **Color I:** Turquoise (134) - for Cherry Stem
» **Color J:** Robin's Egg Blue (151) - for Baby Pacifier

Hook Sizes

» 2mm hook – for Floss Granny Squares
» 2.5mm hook– for Baby Limbs & Pacifier
» 3mm hook – Main hook
» 3.5mm hook– for Hair

Other

» Stitch markers
» Yarn needle
» Stuffing
» Craft Glue
» Pins
» Safety Eyes - Black Oval 3/8" (10mm) x 2
» Scrapbooking Brad - Orange 5/32" (4mm) x 1 - for Nose
» DMC Embroidery Floss – Black – for Facial Features
» Embroidery Needle
» DMC Embroidery Floss (Pink, Baby Blue, Bright Blue, Lilac, Peach & Teal) - for Carrier
» Black sewing thread & sewing needle – for Baby Facial Features

---

FINISHED SIZE
About 7" (18cm) tall

SKILL LEVEL
Intermediate

PATTERN NOTES

The Main hook is used throughout, unless otherwise stated.

When working double crochet rows or rounds, the first ch-2 does not count as the first stitch. The first dc of a row is worked in the last stitch made on the previous row. The first dc of a round is worked in the same stitch as the previous round's join.

Note: *This does not apply to Round 1 of Mini Granny Squares.*

SPECIAL STITCHES

Picot Stitch (picot): Ch 3, sl st in specified stitch.

SAMANTHA

HEAD

Round 1: With MC, make a magic ring, 6 sc in ring. (6 sc)

Round 2: Inc in each st around. (12 sc)

Round 3: [Sc in next st, inc in next st] 6 times. (18 sc)

Round 4: [Sc in next 2 sts, inc in next st] 6 times. (24 sc)

Round 5: [Sc in next 3 sts, inc in next st] 6 times. (30 sc)

Round 6: [Sc in next 4 sts, inc in next st] 6 times. (36 sc)

Round 7: [Sc in next 5 sts, inc in next st] 6 times. (42 sc)

Round 8: [Sc in next 6 sts, inc in next st] 6 times. (48 sc)

Round 9: [Sc in next 7 sts, inc in next st] 6 times. (54 sc)

Round 10: [Sc in next 8 sts, inc in next st] 6 times. (60 sc)

Rounds 11-21: *(11 rounds)* Sc in each st around. (60 sc)

Round 22: [Sc in next 8 sts, inv-dec] 6 times. (54 sc) *(image 1)*

Round 23: [Sc in next 7 sts, inv-dec] 6 times. (48 sc)

Round 24: [Sc in next 6 sts, inv-dec] 6 times. (42 sc)

Add Facial Features:

1. Nose - position brad at front of Head (about 27th stitch on Round 20) and lock in place. *(image 2 & 3)*

2. Eyes - position on Round 19, about 6 stitches from either side of Nose and secure in place. *(image 4 & 5)*

3. Eye Whites - using Color A and yarn needle, make 3-4 vertical straight stitches (the same height as Eyes) to the left of each Eye. Knot and secure the yarn on the inside of the Head. *(image 6)*

Continue crocheting:

Round 25: [Sc in next 5 sts, inv-dec] 6 times. (36 sc)

Round 26: [Sc in next 4 sts, inv-dec] 6 times. (30 sc)

Round 27: [Sc in next 3 sts, inv-dec] 6 times. (24 sc)

Start stuffing Head, adding more as you go.

Round 28: [Sc in next 2 sts, inv-dec] 6 times. (18 sc)

Round 29: [Sc in next st, inv-dec] 6 times. (12 sc)

Round 30: [Inv dec] 6 times. (6 sc) Fasten off.

Close the opening securely and leave a long tail (for Eye Indentations). *(image 7)*

Cheek (Make 2)

Round 1: With Color B, make a magic ring, 6 sc in ring. (6 sc)

Fasten off with Needle Join, leaving a long tail for sewing.

FINISHING THE FACE

Eye Indentations

Using long tail on Head and yarn needle:

1. Bring needle up from base of Head and out next to the nose-side of Eye. *(image 8)*

2. Insert needle in next stitch, bringing it out at base of Head. Gently tug yarn to create a slight indentation at the Eye. *(image 9)*

3. Repeat steps 1 & 2 for other Eye. *(image 10 & 11)*

4. Secure yarn tail with a knot at base of Head and trim excess yarn.

Cheeks - Position the Cheeks below each Eye and sew in place, bringing the yarn out at base of Head. Secure with a knot and trim excess yarn. *(image 12)*

Eyebrows & Mouth

Using Black Embroidery Floss and needle:

1. Bring needle up from base of Head and embroider Eyebrows above each Eye – by making a diagonal straight stitch from Round 16 to Round 17, about 4 stitches long. *(image 13)*

2. After Eyebrows, bring needle down through Head to create a Mouth on Round 22, centered under the Nose – by making a loose horizontal straight stitch, about 4 stitches long, bringing needle out at base of Head. Tie ends in a knot to secure and trim excess yarn. *(image 14)*

3. Optional: Apply glue on Mouth, and use pins to shape the smile while the glue dries. *(image 15 & 16)*

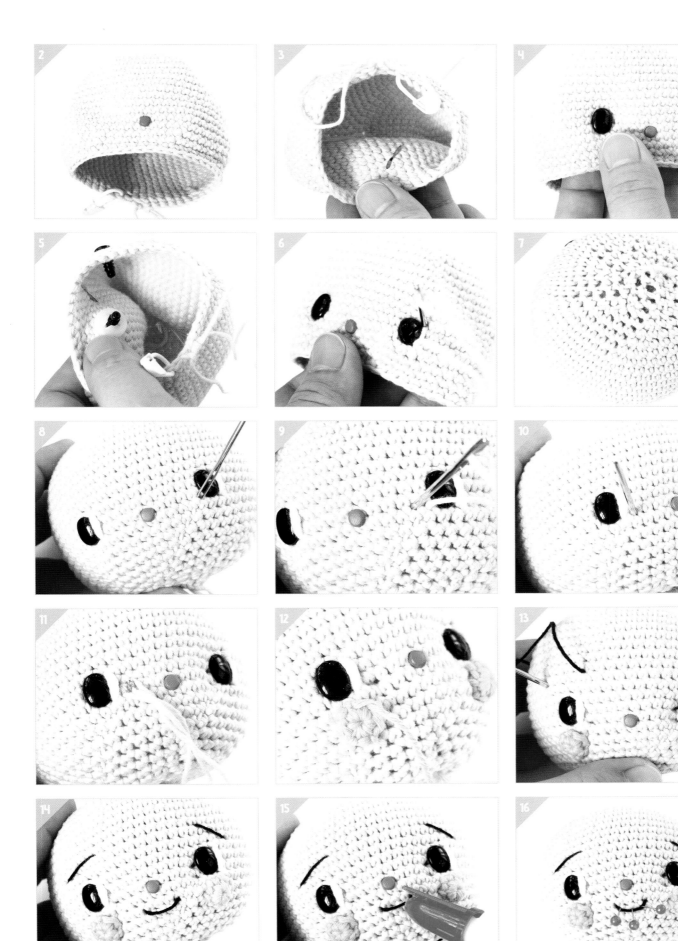

HAIR

Rounds 1-10: With Color C and Hair hook, repeat Rounds 1-10 of the Head.

Rounds 11-13: *(3 rounds)* Sc in each st around. (60 sc)

Work continues in Rows.

Row 1: Dc in the next 18 sts. (18 dc) Leave remaining sts unworked.

Row 2: *(Bangs)* Ch 2, turn, dc in first st, dc in next 7 sts, sl st in next 2 sts, dc in next 8 sts. (16 dc & 2 sl sts) *(image 17)*

Row 3: Working in sides of rows, sc in each of next 2 rows (not counted); working in Round 13, sc in next 42 sts. (42 sc)

Rows 4-8: *(5 rows)* Ch 1, turn, sc in each st across. (42 sc) *(image 18)*

Fasten off, leaving a long tail for sewing.

Ponytail

First Strand: With Color C and Hair hook, ch 20, hdc in 2nd ch from hook, hdc in next 17 ch, (hdc, sl st) in last ch. (19 hdc & 1 sl st)

Next Strand: *Ch 20, hdc in 2nd ch from hook, hdc in next 18 ch, sl st in same last ch on First Strand; repeat from * once more. (3 strands)

Fasten off, leaving a long tail for sewing. *(image 19)*

HAIR TIE

Cherries (Make 2)

With Color H, make a magic ring, 4 sc in ring. (4 sc)

Fasten off, leaving a long tail for sewing.

Stem

With Color I, ch 8. Fasten off, leaving a long tail for sewing.

Attaching Hair

1. Position Hair on Head and sew in place. *(image 20)*

2. Sew Ponytail on top of Head, off-center, near Rounds 3-6 of Hair. *(image 21)*

3. Sew Cherries at base of Ponytail. *(image 22)*

4. Shape Stem into an upside down "V" and sew in place above Cherries. *(image 23)*

BODY

Rounds 1-5: Using Color E, repeat Rounds 1-5 of Head.

Rounds 6-8: *(3 rounds)* Sc in each st around. (30 sc)

Change to Color D.

Round 9: Sc in each st around. (30 sc)

Round 10: Working in **back loops** only, sc in each st around. (30 sc)

Rounds 11-17: *(7 rounds)* Sc in each st around. (30 sc)

Round 18: [Sc in next 3 sts, inv-dec] 6 times. (24 sc)

Fasten off, leaving a long tail for sewing. *(image 24)*

Stuff body firmly.

Skirt

Note: *Round 1 is worked in the unused front loops of Round 9 on Body.*

Round 1: Holding Body upside down, join Color D with standing sc to center back on Round 9; ch 2, 2 dc in each st around; join with sl st to first dc. (60 dc) *(image 25 & 26)*

Rounds 2-3: *(2 rounds)* Ch 2, dc in each st around; join with sl st to first dc. (60 dc)

Change to Color E.

Round 4: *(Frill)* [Sc in next st, picot in same st] around. *(image 27)*

Fasten off and weave in ends.

ARM (Make 2)

Round 1: With MC, make a magic ring, 6 sc in ring. (6 sc)

Round 2: Inc in each st around. (12 sc)

Rounds 3-4: *(2 rounds)* Sc in each st around. (12 sc)

Round 5: [Inv-dec] 3 times, sc in the next 6 sts. (9 sc)

Rounds 6-11: *(6 rounds)* Sc in each st around. (9 sc)

Change to Color D.

Rounds 12-13: *(2 rounds)* Sc in each st around. (9 sc)

Fasten off, leaving a long tail for sewing.

Stuff Arm lightly.

LEG - WITH SHOE (Make 2)

Round 1: With Color G, ch 8; starting in 2nd ch from hook, sc in next 6 ch, 3 sc in last ch, working on other side of starting chain, sc in next 6 ch. (15 sc)

Round 2: Inc in first st, sc in next 6 sts, inc in each of next 2 sts, sc in next 5 sts, inc in last st. (19 sc)

Round 3: Working in **back loops** only, sc in each st around. (19 sc)

Round 4: Sc in each st around. (19 sc) Change to MC.

Round 5: Working in **back loops** only, sc in next 8 sts, [inv-dec] 3 times, sc in next 5 sts. (16 sc) Cut Color G, knot together with starting tail of MC and trim ends.

Round 6: Sc in next 7 sts, [inv-dec] 4 times, sc in last st. (12 sc)

Rounds 7-13: *(7 rounds)* Sc in each st around. (12 sc)

Fasten off, leaving a long tail for sewing.

Stuff legs firmly.

Shoe Strap (Make 2)

With Color G, ch 9.

Fasten off, leaving a long tail for sewing.

Assembling Shoes

Sew Straps across the front of each Shoe, threading the tail ends to the base of Shoe.

Make several stitches with tail ends (to secure the Straps), then thread the tails to the inside of the Shoe and knot the ends together. (image 28)

FINAL DOLL ASSEMBLY

1. Sew Body to finished Head, adding more stuffing before finishing. (image 29)

2. Position Legs and sew in place, adding more stuffing so Doll can stand when propped up against a wall. (image 30)

3. Position the Arms and sew in place. (image 31)

BABY

Baby Head

Round 1: With MC, make a magic ring, 6 sc in ring. (6 sc)

Round 2: Inc in each st around. (12 sc)

Round 3: [Sc in next st, inc in next st] 6 times. (18 sc)

Rounds 4-5: (2 rounds) Sc in each st around. (18 sc)

Round 6: Sc in next 7 sts, 3 sc in next st, sc in next 2 sts, 3 sc in next st, sc in last 7 sts. (22 sc)

Round 7: Sc in each st around. (22 sc)

Round 8: Sc in next 6 sts, [inv-dec] 2 times, sc in next 2 sts, [inv-dec] 2 times, sc in next 6 sts. (18 sc)

Stuff Head firmly.

Round 9: [Sc in next st, inv-dec] 6 times. (12 sc)

Round 10: [Inv-dec] 6 times. (6 sc)

Fasten off, leaving a long tail (to make Eye Indentations).

Baby Body

Round 1: With Color F, make a magic ring, 5 sc in ring. (5 sc)

Round 2: Inc in each st around. (10 sc)

Rounds 3-7: (5 rounds) Sc in each st around. (10 sc)

Fasten off, leaving a long tail for sewing.

Stuff Body firmly.

Baby Arm (Make 2)

Round 1: With MC and Limb hook, make a magic ring, 6 sc in ring. (6 sc)

Round 2: Sc in each st around. (6 sc)

Change to Color F.

Rounds 3-5: (3 rounds) Sc in each st around. (6 sc)

Fasten off, leaving a long tail for sewing.

Baby Leg (Make 2)

Round 1: With Color F and Limb hook, make a magic ring, 7 sc in ring. (7 sc)

Round 2: Sc in each st around. (7 sc)

Round 3: Inv-dec (using first 2 sts), sc in next 5 sts. (6 sc)

Rounds 4-5: (2 rounds) Sc in each st around. (6 sc)

Fasten off, leaving a long tail for sewing.

Pacifier

Round 1: With Color J and Pacifier hook, make a magic ring, 5 sc in ring. (5 sc)

Fasten off, leaving a long tail for sewing.

Assembling Baby

1. Using long tail from Head and yarn needle, make two Eye Indentations on Round 5 with 3 stitches in between them.

2. Using black sewing thread and needle, embroider closed eyelids (with eyelashes) on the Head. (image 32)

3. Sew Pacifier between the Eyes.

4. With Color B, embroider 2-3 straight lines under the Eyes for Cheeks. (image 33)

5. Sew Body onto Head.

6. Sew on Arms and Legs. (image 34)

BABY CARRIER

Mini Granny Squares (Make 6 – 1 in each Floss color)

Round 1: With Floss Color and Floss hook, make a magic ring, 5 sc in ring. (5 sc)

Round 2: Ch 3 (counts as first dc), working in center of sc-ring, 2 dc in ring, ch 2, [3 dc in ring, ch 2] 3 times; join with sl st to first dc (3rd ch of beg ch-3). (image 35)

Change to Color E and Main hook. (cut Floss & weave in ends)

Round 3: Ch 1, *(2 sc, ch 1, 3 sc, ch 1) in next ch 2 sp; repeat from * 3 times more; join with sl st to first sc.

Fasten off, leaving a long tail for sewing. (image 36 & 37)

Joining Granny Squares

Using long tails and yarn needle, working in **back loops** only, whipstitch granny squares together, making a block of 3 squares by 2 squares. (image 38 & 39)

Edging & Straps

Using Color E and Main hook, make a standing sc in any corner ch-1 sp, *ch 35, starting in 2nd ch from hook, sc in each ch across (strap made). (34 sc)*

Starting on short side, sc in each st across to corner, 2 sc in corner ch-1 sp; working across long side, sc in each st across to corner, 2 sc in corner ch-1 sp; working in other short side, sc in each st across to corner.

Repeat from * to * once more.

Working across other long side, sc in each st across. (image 40)

Fasten off and weave in ends

Finishing Baby Carrier

1. Sew the end of each Strap to the opposite corner, making an "X". Secure and fasten off. (image 41)

2. Slip Baby Carrier over Doll. (image 42)

3. Place Baby in Baby Carrier. (image 43)

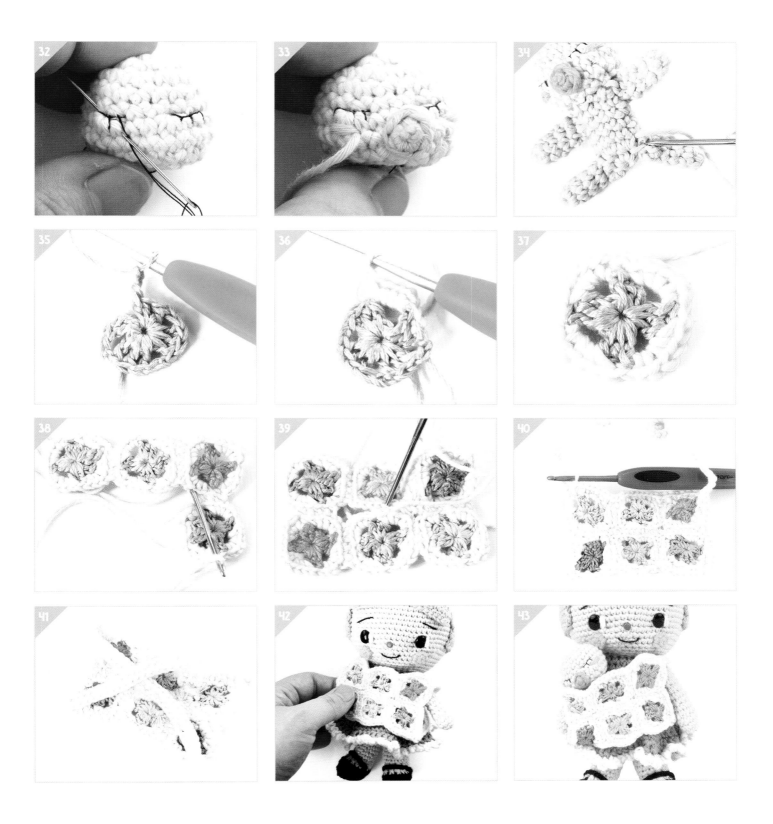